To My Parents

Sri Subrahmanya Vara Prasad & Smt Sri Lakshmi

&

To the Divine Force, That Triggered This Effort

Table of Contents

Science and Philosophy

Philosophy starts where the evidence stops. It goes well beyond the immediate facts and stretches the imaginative power. The commonality between Science and Philosophy is that both agree to disagree and allow new ways of looking at things. This adds beauty to both fields. Similar to the fact that every scientific theory opens up new avenues for further imagination, every Philosophical school trigger multiple branches. India is home to many such schools of Philosophy which emerged over her thousands of years of civilization. This book tries to bring out the gist of such schools and the underlying unity among them.

As per modern-day science, the universe that we see is the result of a big bang that took place approximately 1400 Crore years ago. The universe has innumerable galaxies. Each galaxy has innumerable stars. Our galaxy is named as Milky way which is over 1.5 lakh light-years across. The universe undergoes cyclic expansion and contraction leading to the collapse of mass into a tiny point from where another cycle of creation starts through one more bang. Mathematical probability predicts that there is a possibility of the existence of wise species like humans and habitable solar systems in far-off galaxies. Science uses the biggest possible space observatories and long voyaging spaceships to locate the habitable worlds outside our solar systems. On the other hand, Philosophy believes that such habitable worlds are around us. They are too subtler to see and feel with our senses. One needs to cultivate the Divine vision (Divya Chakshu) to behold such realms.

Science has made rigorous efforts to understand the universe. As it stands today, the general opinion of science is that what we see, and feel is only 5% of the universe. There is a hidden 95% of the universe which includes dark matter and dark energy. These two are ensuring that the universe is not collapsing. This dark matter does not absorb light and does not interact with electromagnetic waves, yet it has a gravitational effect. ***Dark matter cannot be wet by water, blown by the wind, cut by a knife, or seen using physical eyes.*** Scientists mathematically predicted that the universe has around 27% dark matter. Dark energy, on the other hand, makes up around 68% of the universe and is responsible for the motion of galaxies, and the expansion of Space-Time. In essence behind the curtains there is mass and energy which is projecting and preserving the universe that we see. It may take many years for scientists to get hold of a preliminary glimpse of the invisible mass and energy that are influencing the universe.

Thousands of years back, Indians started to explore the features of the invisible mass and energy that is controlling the universe. Over the generations, they contemplated how to sharpen their intellect to peep into the hidden mass and energy that is behind us. With their sharpened intellect Indians have had glimpses of attributes of invisible matter and invisible energy. They named the inviable matter Prakriti (Mother Nature) and invisible energy as Paramatma (Super Soul or Maheswara). They composed hymns to praise and please invisible Mass and Energy.

They learned the art of tapping the required boons from them. They mastered the art of seeking the answers from the invisible matter and energy on intriguing questions that rattled human minds. They understood that there is something behind the curtains which is affectionately gesturing us to its realms of peace and tranquility. They understood that the one who is the cause of this universe is acting as an onlooker of our journey. The time and space that are constraining us are not effective in the realms of the onlooker. Indians realized that the Paramatma seats himself in the timeless world. He is beginningless.

Science predicts that around 1400 crore years back time and space started with the big bang. The question of what existed ahead of the big bang is irrelevant to science as time does not exist before the big bang. Like philosophy fails to provide logic to the seekers beyond certain limits but rather encourages them to explore on their own, Science also cannot give a convincing answer on what lies ahead of the big bang. Whether the absence of time before the big bang automatically indicates the absence of all other things. It leaves space for individuals to propose logical theories to enrich the available knowledge.

Science is making serious efforts to explain certain aspects of the universe using both classical physics and quantum physics. As it stands today, none of these schools of Physics can explain the origin and nature of the universe in its totality. Each school fails to explain one or other features of the energies and attributes of the universe. The unification of these two schools of physics is the biggest challenge for present-day science. The unification of these two schools is possible only with a radical relook at the basics of science. Part of Physics is proposing such a radical relook and trying to circumvent the issue by proposing that, time what we feel is psychological time. There is evidence for the non-existence of time, where the world can nonetheless be experienced. Physics today is glaring at the myth of time and trying to understand the concepts of timeless worlds. Concepts of multiple and parallel worlds and the illusion of motion proposed by quantum physics are the revolutionary concepts that are shaking the fundamental understanding of the universe. To a common man, these concepts sound illogical, but any learned scholar of modern science agrees with the feasibility of such radical concepts. So are many concepts in Philosophy.

Quantum physics proposes that the universe in which we live has intentionally created the wise species like human beings as it wants to see whether these wise men and women can look back and feel those present behind the curtains. This emerging school of physics is called Anthro Physics. A section of quantum physics proposes that, the cat that jumps off the table and the one that lands are different, as at every moment the mass is disappearing into the dark matter and reappearing back afresh. In the years to come, quantum physics will make possible 'what today we believe as impossible or myth'. For such deep scientific churning, stable world order free from wars and calamities is essential. From a stable and prosperous society, many scientific and literary advances can spring up which can make life more comfortable and meaningful. The right philosophy that promotes peace and harmony in society can enable this to happen.

On the contrary, to utilise the platform provided by stable and prosperous societies for deep explorations into the field of science and art, individuals should be ambitious, mature, accommodative and innovative. Such a genre of individuals cannot be nurtured by science. It needs the support of arts at large and positive philosophy in particular. The philosophy should be such that, it should be able to influence our thinking, influence our actions, influence the way we react to success and failures, and influence our goals in life. It should not promote hatred and narrow thinking. It should never declare what is right and wrong. It should make the individuals choose the right path through their blossomed intellect, rather than through stereotype stories. If any philosophical school declares that, the path pronounced by it is the only path for wisdom and the rest of the paths lead to hell, it can be inferred that it is an unscientific path leading to narrow thinking. Such a philosophy cannot enable the individual and society to be progressive and accommodative. Both classical physics and quantum physics are correct, but both don't go with each other in their approach. Similarly, many philosophical schools that have evolved are right in their approach yet may not be matching with the approach of other schools of philosophy. Many philosophical schools that have evolved across the globe enriched the human race over the past thousands of years. India is home to such philosophical schools that are united in their outlook towards the purpose of life yet divided in their practices. The purpose of all these philosophical schools is to elevate the soul to higher realms and behold the creator and onlooker of the universe. All philosophical schools agreed on the in-principal existence of the Divine Trinity, they are Soul (Jeevatma), Prakriti (Nature which is visible and invisible) and Paramatma (Super soul). As mentioned, Prakriti has its parlance to the dark or invisible matter and Paramatma has its parlance with invisible energy. Readers of this book are requested to understand that author is not trying to prove the scientific validity of the Indian philosophy but rather, stressing the point that, the horizons of science are the fertile fields for philosophical thoughts. It allows the human imagination to travel ahead of time, it filters the imagination into logical extrapolations, and it compiles the aggregates of logical thoughts into the guidebook for practice thus defining the contours for a wise journey further. In general, the end goal of any philosophy is to understand the purpose of life. It promotes compassion and truthfulness. Thus, it elevates the individual.

As the Paramatma is believed to be above the weaknesses and shortcomings that humans possess, it becomes essential for anyone who is treading the path to behold Paramatma, to make themselves eligible to enter the realms of Paramatma by shedding the shortcomings. Thus, the advantage of association with any positive philosophical school is that it enables individuals to introspect on the weak links in their attitude and outlook. Thus, it gives a soothing feeling to the mind and enables it to focus on the right things. Once the mind learns the art of calming itself, it can trigger the urge to dive deep into the unexplored potentials of human imagination through single-pointed contemplation. The outcome of such contemplation with blossomed intellect is that it enables the individual to visualize the realms which lie beyond the visualization of an agitating mind. In essence, while science explores the secrets of the universe through the intuitive ability of individual scientists assisted by external tools, philosophy enables us to feel the secrets of the universe by sharpening the intuitive ability of internal tools of the body. Thus, in philosophy, the personality of the individual becomes the tool for exploring the secrets of the universe, as it conditions our personality for such a journey. This conditioning encompasses conditioning five sensory organs, mind, attitude, outlook and most importantly how we react to the results of our actions.

Indian philosophy is one of the oldest philosophies, over time it has grown into many branches. Every Indian is knowingly or unknowingly influenced by one or the other philosophical schools. This book brings out the essence of Indian philosophy through an unbiased exploration of various branches of religious schools that thrived in this sacred land. Each of the religious schools mentioned in this book can invoke divinity within us. Even a little effort in this direction can save individuals from the perils of worldly accidents. These religious schools can ensure a peaceful life and a prosperous society. *Hence this book is named "Svalpamapi" which means even a small Dharmic effort can save us from great perils (The word "Svalpamapi" is taken from the Bhagavad Gita Chapter II: Sloka 40).*

The main contents of the text written in this book are taken from Bhagavad Gita, Patanjali Yoga sutras and Upanishads. To the best of my ability, I tried to bring out the essence of prominent philosophical schools of India. This book aims to redefine the multifaceted philosophical thoughts of India and the underlying unity among them using the Bhagavad Gita and Patanjali Yoga Sutras as guiding lights. Presenting the Bhagavad Gita and other sacred texts of India in an easily comprehendible manner for the present generation is also one of the aims of this book.

Those who are interested to study further the concepts of physics discussed in this chapter can refer to the following books.

i) *Dark Matter & Dark Energy. The Hidden 95% of the Universe* by Brian Clegg. ICON Books,2019

ii) *The Theory of Every Thing. The Origin and the Fate of the Universe* by Stephen Hawkings. JAICO Books, 2009

iii) *Brief Answers to the Big Questions* by Stephen Hawkings, John Murray and Publishers, 2018.

iv) *The End of Time: The Next Revolution in Physics* by Julian Barbour, Oxford University Press,2001.

v) *Code Name God. The Spiritual Odyssey of a Man of Science* by Mani Bhaumik. Penguin India 2006.

Overview of Chapters

The First chapter deals with 'Shat Darshanas' which means six philosophies. They deal with six different schools of Indian philosophical thought. They define the boundaries for logical debate between scholars. They don't allow illogical statements on the existence of the Soul (Jeevatma) or Super soul (Paramatma) and other religious concepts. Basic principles of these six schools namely Nyaya, Vaiseshika, Sankhya, Yoga, Purva Mimamsa & Uttara Mimamsa (Vedanta) are summarised in this chapter. This chapter shows how various religious schools evolved in India around differing logical views on the existence of supernature. It is generally believed that, without the knowledge of Shat Darshanas, no one can comprehend the true meaning of Vedas, Upanishads and especially the Bhagavad Gita. Hence this chapter is introduced as the first chapter.

This chapter brings out how Sankhya and Vedanta have taken different sides on their views regarding the Jeevatma, Prakriti and Paramatma. This chapter sets the stage for readers to understand, how differing views of Sankhya and Vedanta lead to the evolution of various sects in Hinduism and how Bhagavad Gita approved both schools thereby accepting the multiple philosophical paths to reach the same goal.

The second chapter of this book contains questions and answers. This chapter is created for easy comprehension of various concepts that frequently rattles the mind of spiritual seekers. It includes the most recurring questions of philosophy and the authentic answer for those questions based on the inferences from the Bhagavad Gita & Patanjali Yoga Sutras.

The third chapter is on Genesis of the Universe. It brings out Vedic and Bhagavad Gita's views on how creation started. Who was behind the creation, and what is the purpose of creation?

The fourth chapter is the most comprehensive summary of various sects of Indian philosophy and practice. This chapter starts with a basic introduction to Sankhya from the perspective of the Bhagavad Gita and then descends to present-day practices of various sects of Hinduism. It brings out the underlying philosophy behind each sect. This chapter is titled "Sankhya, Vedanta and the Divine Trinity: Multiple Paths with One Goal". It starts with a detailed discussion on Sankhya. Then it brings out the essence of Bhagavad Gita's view on Jeevatma, Prakriti and Paramatma. These three together are identified as the Divine trinity. Then elaborate discussions were made on how subtle differences in understanding the Divine trinity and the difference of opinions on the state of liberation (Moksha) led to the formation of various sects in Hinduism. Various philosophical schools that were discussed include Dualistic, Non-Dualistic schools, and Vaishnavite schools which include Ramanuja's tradition, Madhwa Tradition, Vallabh Charya tradition, Vaikhanasa, ISCKON etc.., Discussions on Saivitic Schools covered Kashmiri Saivism, Pasupata Saivism/Srouta Saivism, Veera Saivism, Lingayat Saivism, Nadh Saivism & Saiva Siddhanta of Tamil lands. This chapter also includes discussions on Sakta school, Sun worship (Saura Scholl), Ganapatya school and Skanda/Karthikeya school. The philosophy of each of these schools, in terms of their take on Jeevatma, Prakriti and Paramatma was discussed in detail. Concepts of Sikhism, Buddhism and Jainism are also discussed at the end to give a comprehensive view of various religious schools evolved in India. How sacred 'OM' forms the joining thread for all the philosophies that evolved in India is elaborated towards the end of the chapter.

The fifth chapter deals with various Austerities (Tapa) for Senses and Significance of Right Association recommended by Bhagavad Gita. It brings out the consequences of allowing uncontrolled sensual pleasures. It emphasizes that the mind should be the master of the senses. The significance of the right association, and how to identify the right association are discussed in this chapter. This chapter brings out the emphasis of the Bhagavad Gita on controlling the senses as the primary requirement to prosper in physical or spiritual life.

The sixth chapter deals with Sin. It defines what is Sin. It identifies sin at three different levels namely physical, mental and spiritual levels. It lists the consequences of committing sin. It also brings out the myths associated with sin. It ends with a discussion on methods to wash off sins.

The Seventh chapter deals with levels of consciousness. This chapter recommends to seekers identify themselves as not a mere body but rather as a conscious force having the ability to expand the consciousness in an unbound manner. How to expand the consciousness to behold the vastness of Jeevatma and Paramatma through Yogic practices is discussed in this chapter.

The eighth chapter deals with righteousness recommended by religion and righteousness recommended for religion. As part of righteousness defined by religion, extracts from the Bhagavad Gita on austerities of Body, Mind, Action & Intellect were discussed. These austerities are essential for every individual irrespective of their spiritual inclination. These austerities are recommended even for those who are not aiming at spiritual upliftment. This is because these practices can ensure purposeful life. This chapter also deals with a discussion on what is righteousness for the religion. It emphasizes that, when there is a conflict between religious thoughts and basic human values, the latter should get priority.

The ninth chapter brings out the basic essence of three primitive qualities (primitive energies of nature) namely Satvik, Rajasik and Tamasik. It classifies various types of thoughts and actions into three categories. How these qualities affect the present life and the life after death is discussed in this chapter. How to utilise these primitive energies of nature to overcome the nest of illusion (Maya) is discussed in this chapter.

The tenth chapter contains concluding remarks. It lists out the most essential practices one should never ignore.

The eleventh Chapter contains thirty-two selected slokas from Bhagavad Gita with simple meanings. These slokas can give the overall essence of the Bhagavad Gita. These thirty-two slokas are worth memorizing as they can help to mould our personality.

Note for the Readers: Every effort is made to write this book without deviating from the authentic essence of Shat Darshanas, Bhagavad Gita, Patanjali Yoga Sutras, Upanishads & Vedic Hymns. Every chapter in this book is the essence of many quotes from these standard texts. Wherever readers find merit in this book, the credit goes to the seers who have built these noble concepts over generations. Wherever there are short-comings or wrong interpretations it is because of my ignorance. I am ready to correct it. Those who wish to suggest any corrections or improvements are requested to convey the same through email at drivatur-isrikanth@gmail.com. I will try to accommodate all suggestions in the subsequent editions.

For each of the concepts taken from the Bhagavad Gita, references to the corresponding Chapter and corresponding Slokas are given in the parenthesis. For instance, reference (Gita III.4) is to be understood as the fourth shloka of the third chapter of Bhagavad Gita, and reference (Gita II.4-6) should be understood as Slokas 4 to 6 from Chapter 2 of Bhagavad Gita. Wherever the references are made from Patanjali Yoga sutras, Upanishads & Vedic texts full reference is given at the same place in the text.

Chapter I

Six Schools of Philosophy: The Platform for Logical Debate

Prelude: To understand religious schools that evolved in the sacred land of India, one needs to understand the common threads of various Philosophies that emerged from this land. Though Vedas and Upanishads are the oldest philosophical texts, many philosophies like Jainism, Buddhism etc. evolved which have their own sacred texts. However, the common platform for all these philosophies is 'shat darshans' which provides a platform for logical debate on spiritualism. They are Nyaya, Vaiseshika, Sankhya, Yoga, Purva Mimamsa and Uttara Mimamsa.

A philosophical argument between Adi Shankaracharya (depicted on the right side) and Mandana Mishra under the

supervision of Ubhaya Bharati. In this historically famous argument, Adi Sankara argued in favor of Uttara Mimamsa and Mandana Mishra argued in favor of Purva Mimamsa.

These six schools together are called as 'Shat Darshanas' which ensured that logic and reasoning are inbuilt into religious philosophy and ensured that religion is open for debate. To understand the Bhagavad Gita and other Upanishads basic knowledge of Shat Darshanas is required. This chapter is an attempt to condition the readers with a basic introduction to Shat Darshanas which is the platform for logical debate for scholars.

Six Schools for Logical Debate: First among the six schools of Indian thought is '**Nyaya**'. It was propounded by Sage Gautama. Nyaya says that any theory that is proposed should not deviate from the properties of the matter and physically verifiable facts. Nyaya allows four types of logic for debate. They are 'direct evidence *(Pratyaksha)*' that is, one which can be sensed or grasped by senses. 'Inference' *(Anumana)* from the direct evidence is the second allowed type of logic. For example, when smoke is seen on a hilltop, it can be inferred that there is fire though we do not see fire. Here fire is a possibility or inference (Sadhya) and smoke is the indication (Linga). The relationship between fire and smoke is something inseparable (Avinabhava). Inference derived from inseparable entities is allowed for debate. Comparative evidence *(Upamana)* is the third allowed logic. For instance, a cow (which everyone sees) can be used to explain an animal in the forest (which everyone doesn't get a chance to see). The fourth allowed logic in the debate is the words of a learned person *(Aptavakya),* which is something experienced by a learned person through his knowledge. Thus, a total of four types of logics are allowed by Nyaya school in establishing any philosophy.

Vaiseshika is the second in line of six schools of Indian thought. It was promoted by Sage 'Kanada'. It deals with the origin and existence of the universe. As per this school, everything in this universe is made up of atoms which are the smallest building blocks of matter. Brahman or Brahma (Super soul) adds the consciousness aspect to the universe. This school states that each type of matter is associated with a particular quality (Gunas).

Sensory organs can feel matter. But internally some entity should be coordinating the external world with consciousness which is named Manah (Mind). *As per this school since we can feel happiness, sorrow, urge (to do or learn) etc. which are not made up of physical atoms, yet they are felt by us, hence, there should be something which is not made up of physical matter which is triggering and receiving these feeling. That entity which is not made up of matter yet feeling the pleasures and pains is Jeevatma (Soul).* Since the body is made up of matter, and Jeevatma (Soul) is not made up of matter, it should be different from the body. Since the feelings of each individual are different, Jeevatmas present in each body should have been different. As per this school evolution which involves interaction of atoms or energies to create something never happens without a purpose. So, there should be a purpose for each Jeevatma. Since the visible matter (mass) is governed by certain physical laws, in a similar manner the invisible

Jeevatmas also should be following laws governed by some invisible entity. That is Paramatma or Super soul.

This school further proposes that knowledge or wisdom (Gnana) can't exist without 'I' (Feeling of 'I am'). Hence wisdom is a quality which can't have independent existence without 'Jeevatma'. So Jeevatma should be above the wisdom derived from the Prakritic tools. That pure consciousness of 'I'ness is defined as Jeevatma (Soul) by Vaiseshika. Nyaya and Vaiseshika schools go hand in hand with minor differences in the allowed domain of evidence for the logical debate.

As per these schools, Action (Karma) need matter and quality (three primitive energies of nature namely Satva, Raja and Tama). However, one who is acting is different from matter and energy though it cannot get expressed without these. On the other hand, qualities (Satva, Raja, Tamas) and matter cannot act themselves unless there is someone to act using them as a tool. Jeevatma is the one which acts using these tools. These tools are with Prakriti. Thus, the entire universe is acting due to the interaction of Jeevatma and Prakriti. As per this school, the universe that we see is the result of the mixing up of three primitive energies with the matter at different proportions with the consciousness of Jeevatma. Among the five prime elements of creation, the first four are limited in their spread, yet the fifth one that is space is universal and infinite. Since the mixing up of matter of the first four elements is not random but rather purposeful and fruitful to make the manifested world, thus there should be a limited cause behind this. This is because, without conscious cause, action can't happen and without someone to act matter and energies of Prakriti (Satva, Raja and Tama) can't act on themselves in such an organised manner. In the same manner for the spread of infinite space and time (the fifth prime element of Prakriti), there should be a cause and there should be someone who is acting behind this cause. He is Paramatma who should be subtler than space and larger than the infinite universe. This is how Nyaya and Vaiseshika scholars debate the existence of Jeevatma and Paramatma.

The third school of philosophy is **Sankhya** which was propounded by Sage Kapila. It revolves around the concept of Prakriti (Matter, Creative energy) and Purusha (Soul) and Purushottam or Paramatma (Super soul or the seed soul). These three together form the Divine Trinity. Sankhya proposes that Paramatma is the special soul who was never touched by Klesa (Pain) or Karma (Activity). It is the omniscient consciousness. Prakriti (Mother Nature) is the nourishing source for the Jeevatmas. It provides material and energy (three primitive energies in the form of Satvik, Rajasik and Tamasik) tools for the survival and evolution of Jeevatmas. On the other hand, Jeevatmas are the individual souls which were seeded by Paramatma at the beginning of the creation. They have come under the charm of Prakriti. They need to evolve using the Prakritic tools to a level where they are no more under the constraints of Prakriti and are thus liberated from the repeated cycles of manifestations (birth and death). A more elaborate discussion on Sankhya is made in chapter IV. **Yoga** is the fourth school of the orthodox Indian system which teaches how to unite the Soul (Jeevatma) with the Super soul through meditative contemplation. It also includes methods on how to

18

condition the body and mind to behold the ultimate truth. Sankhya provides the metaphysical background for the elevation of Jeevatma whereas Yoga teaches the methods and practices to elevate the Jeevatma. Sankhya and Yoga go hand in hand in their philosophical principles.

Purva Mimamsa is the fifth school of Indian Philosophy which was promoted by Sage Jaimini. Sage Badarayana is also one of the foremost proponents of this school. This school allows all four types of logic and reasoning that were allowed by Nyaya School. In addition to it, this school proposed two more allowed logics for debate. They are Extrapolation of fact *(Ardhapatti)* and Non-perception (*Anupalabdhi*) or impossibility of something through extrapolation of facts. Ardhaptti infers many possible statements from one fact. For instance, if someone says "He is not at home", that can be extrapolated as "He has gone out", "He is alive" etc. The difference between the second logic which is inference (Anumana pramana) and the Ardhapatti is that the former deals with certainty (like if there is smoke, there must be fire), whereas the latter indicates only possibility but not certainty. Thus, the possibility is the basis of Ardhapatti. The last of the six allowed logics of this school is certainty in the impossibility of something *(Anupalabdhi)*

Purva Mimamsa believes in the concept of "Vedas as authorless (apourisheya) and self-illuminating knowledge evolved on their own". So, Vedas are not constrained by any of the six logics and are thus infallible. On the other hand, the Vedanta school, the last one among the six schools of thought proposes that Vedas have come out from the Paramatma. Purva Mimamsa goes deep into the six proposed logics. As per this school, even the direct evidence can get contaminated or may get constrained by the person who is viewing or experiencing it. Like a just-born baby can't distinguish various facets of matter around him, similarly if the Knower (Gyata) is not able to use his tools of cognition, memory (smriti) and discretion (viveka) properly he may derive incomplete knowledge or wrong perception. Hence the perception of the knower may change, though the one that is to be perceived may be the same. One that is to be perceived is true knowledge. Thus, the true existence of matter (padardha) is sensitive to the knower whereas the knowledge is not. Thus, it differentiates various levels of direct evidence. This school proposes that to properly transmit whatever knowledge that was gained, proper pronunciation should be used. Thus, Mimamsa school stressed on the proper way of chanting Vedas and other scriptures. Purva Mimamsa goes along with Nyaya and Sankhya in accepting the reality of the world. It does not accept the world we see as an illusion. Purva Mimamsa also agrees in 'Satkaryavada' that is believing in the fact that visible objects are a combination of matter and energy at different proportions. 'Law of Karma' is one of the important points substantiated by Purva Mimamsa.

The most debated question that was raised by Purva Mimamsa was that, whether the 'Law of Karma' can be escaped with the blessings of Paramatma or not. Purva Mimamsa proposed that the results of action (called Apurva) follow the Jeevatma till the Jeevatma experiences them in the form of pleasures or pains. As per Purva Mimamsa school, the Law of Karma of the individuals can give results and thus capable of administering the world. ***Thus, the role of Paramatma is limited as Paramatma cannot deviate from the Law of Karma. If he does deviate, it shows his partiality and questions his unbiased nature. As per this school, questioning the "Law of Karma" is questioning the authenticity of Vedas.*** The emphasis on the Law of Karma is so pronounced in this school that, it has even given a backseat to Paramatma. This is because the role of Paramatma is diluting the "Law of Karma". Thus, it is silent on the role of Paramatma in administering the universe.

Uttara Mimamsa is the last of the six orthodox schools. It is also known as **Vedanta**. It has strongly refuted the Purva Mimamsa school on its rigid view on the "Law of Karma and its ambiguous stand on the role of Paramatma in administering the universe". In Vedic texts and Upanishads Paramatma was hailed as the one who can wash all the sins of individuals. At the same time, they also upheld the concept of the Law of Karma. To bring coherence between these two concepts, Vedanta proposed that, the world we see is an illusion. We feel it is real due to ignorance. As long as we are ignorant, we feel the pleasures and pains and thus bound by the Law of Karma. Those who seek the helping hand of the Almighty will receive the wisdom which dispels ignorance. It is like waking up from a dream into reality. Those who woke up from the dream, are not bound by the pleasures and pains experienced in the dream and also not bound by activities done in the dream. Thus, it is possible to make Law of Karma irrelevant by acquiring the true wisdom.

As long as ignorance of ego and "I" ness exists, the Law of Karma will catch up, once the illusion of "I" ness vanishes and dissolves in Paramatma, the Law of Karma vanishes.

Thus, Vedanta brought coherence between the Law of Karma and the compassionate Paramatma. The Focus of Vedanta is more on Upanishads (the latter part of Vedas) rather than on the former part of Vedas which deals with Yagnas (sacred immolation with Vedic chants). Vedanta is so popular among the masses that, it has become a synonym for Indian Philosophy. This is because many great seers have travelled the length and breadth of India and abroad preaching various aspects of Vedanta. Advaita Vedanta (Non-dualistic school of Vedanta), Dwaita Vedanta (Dualistic School), Visistadwaita (Qualified monism) etc.-are part of Vedantic schools of Philosophy. A more elaborate discussion of Vedanta is made in Chapter IV of this book.

Thus, one needs to understand that, Indian Philosophy is open for debate and questioning. It stresses rational thinking and a logical understanding of Supernature using natural tools. Concepts of all six schools of rational thinking mentioned above can be seen in the Bhagavad Gita which repeatedly emphasises that all schools will lead to the same source of ultimate knowledge. Thus, Bhagavad Gita promoted individuals to explore their inner selves through rational thinking. For those who feel they cannot pursue any of these schools, rather wish to surrender themselves thereby leaving the responsibility on Almighty himself, Bhagavad Gita proposes complete surrender (Gita XVIII:66). However, to experience progress through any of these paths, one needs to condition his

22

body and mind. Bhagavad Gita discourses on the need for such conditioning and methods to be practised to make the body and mind ready to behold the Almighty.

One who wants to understand the Bhagavad Gita and Upanishads should be familiar with the concepts and terminology used in the Shat Darshanas. The words like Prakriti, Purusha, Paramatma, Para, Parapara, Apara (lowest and generic as per Nyaya), Hetu (cause), Guans (prime qualities and energies of nature), Dravya, Klesa, Ichha, Buddhi, Manah etc used in Bhagavad Gita should be understood based on the contextual similarity with these six schools. Similarly, the relation between the Gunas with nature, Jeevatma with Karma (action) etc. proposed by Bhagavad Gita can't be understood in totality without having the basic knowledge of these schools.

There are some slokas in Bhagavad Gita which at first glance looks to contradict each other. For instance, the question of whether our destiny is pre-decided. (See slokas chapter III;27 to 29) or we are free to choose our destiny? (For instance, see the Slokas Chapter V:5 &15). While the former set of slokas can be interpreted from the rigid Law of Karma proposed by Purva Mimamsa, the latter set of slokas can be easily comprehended from the Vedanta which agrees on the grace of Paramatma to lift us from the clutches of the Law of Karma (See Slokas Chapter XVIII:66, IX 27-31). This is because Paramatma is above the Law of Karma (Gita IV:14). Many seekers have attained such a state of freedom from the Law of Karma by surrendering the ego (Gita IV:15). There are some Bhagavad Gita slokas which promote the concept of 'we are not doer, rather Prakriti is the doer' (from Chapter III:21 &22). It can be better understood from Nyaya and Vaiseshika Philosophy. Similarly, Sloka III:30 can be better understood from the Nyaya perspective.

Bhagavad Gita simplified the Vedanta and brought coherence between the Sankhya and Vedanta. It is difficult to have a Vedantic view of visualising the world as delusion by a majority of the people. However, it is easy to surrender the ego ("I" ness) and seek refuge at the feet of Paramatma which is sufficient to come out of the "Law of Karma". Thus, Bhagavad Gita moved one step ahead towards the common man who doesn't have the energy and time to bog down into the deep philosophy. *In other words, Paramatma himself moved close to the common man and stretched his helping hand. It is for us to make use of it (Gita XVIII:66)*

One needs to understand that the six schools of philosophy mentioned above are not contradictions, but rather subtle differences in perceptions. Bhagavad Gita is upholding all six schools of rational thinking, for that matter any school of rational thinking. It is the stress on rational thinking and logical debate that makes the Bhagavad Gita, and the Religions that have evolved in the sacred land of India special.

Jainism and Buddhism though differ in their perspective on the supremacy of Vedas, yet they have not deviated much from the Nyaya, Vaiseshika, Sankhya and Mimamsa when debating about the existence of Jeevatma and Paramatma. Their views may differ from other religious schools but the logical platform on which they debate is the same. Thus, six orthodox schools of Indian philosophy acted as a common platform for intellectual debate over thousands of years in this sacred land.

Over thousands of years, concepts of the above schools got intermingled among the masses. A common Hindu carries the beliefs of all the above-mentioned schools of thought. For example, he believes in Sankhya where the concept of Prakriti and Purush is dominant. Siva Kalyan i.e., the concept of the Marriage Ceremony of Lord Siva with Paravati and conducting marriage ritual every year on the day of Siva Ratri, Seeta Rama Kalyan i.e. the concept of Marriage of Lord Rama with Sita, conducted every year by devotees on the day of Sri Rama Navami are in essence recognition of Prakriti as mother and Purusha as father and celebrating their oneness and seeking their blessings. Hindus also believe in Yoga as a method to elevate the self. They also believe in Purva Mimamsa thereby carrying the concept of the Law of Karma. At the same time, common Hindus also believe in Uttara Mimamsa or Vedanta which refuted Purva Mimamsa and Yoga. Deep philosophical thoughts of these schools and subtle differences between them may not be relevant to all, except for those who want to dwell deep into Indian Philosophy. Every era necessitates society to change and also lifestyles to change. However, the change in lifestyle should not come at a cost of loss of the wisdom acquired over the ages. Day-to-day practices can be changed as per the place of living or type of profession, but the philosophical thought that makes up the men and women of society should not change drastically. This ensures subtle yet deep-rooted unity in society. Keeping this in mind, various writers have brought out innumerable books over many centuries. They redefined the philosophy of the land in a manner which is easy to comprehend by the masses of their generation. This book is one such effort.

Re-emphasizing the above fact, social conditions are dynamic. The ever-changing social system which includes the education system, economic system, political system etc. influences the lifestyle of individuals. Though the change is unavoidable, the underlying noble thoughts that bring unity in society on the goal and purpose of life need to be upheld. The present generation has to preserve, refine and hand it over to the next generation in a way that can be comprehended and carried forward. This ensures the continuity of the Soul of Society. This book is an attempt to portray different facets of Indian philosophy and religious schools and the underlying unity among them. Though Bhagavad Gita is widely referred to in this book, it encompasses the concepts of Patanjali Yoga Sutras and other Upanishads.

Conclusion: Six Schools of the logical debate agreed on the existence of Jeevatma, Prakriti and Paramatma. Except for Uttara Mimamsa (Vedanta) rest all branches of Shat Darshanas agreed with the Sankhya school on the concept of liberation (Moksha) which states the Prakriti (world) is real, but it is irrelevant for the Jeevatmas which have got liberated. Liberated Jeevatma becomes equal to Paramatma but retains its original identity. On the other hand, Vedanta proposed that the world we see is a delusion and we feel it as real due to the false identification of Jeevatma with the body. In the state of liberation, Jeevatma merges with Paramatma and losses its own identity. These differing views of

26

Sankhya and Vedanta lead to the evolution of various subsects in Hinduism. This aspect will be taken forward in the next chapters with the Bhagavad Gita teachings and Patanjali Yoga Sutras as the central theme to show how various subsects of Hinduism evolved around this differing view of Sankhya and Vedanta on the reality of the world and state of liberation

Chapter II

Simple Answers to Complex Questions

Prelude: Many questions on philosophy have rattled human minds since time immemorial. Even when Lord Krishna was discoursing Arjuna, the latter lamented that he got confused with many schools of philosophy. He requested simple answers to complex questions that he has got (Gita III:2). This chapter brings out such complex questions that arise in everyone's mind with the authentic answers for such questions taken from the sacred text of Bhagavad Gita & Patanjali Yoga Sutras. This chapter conditions the readers to understand the contents of the remaining chapters of this book

Those students who tuned their hearts with Guru, need not ask questions as Guru answers all questions through the silent transmission of knowledge (Ref: Hymns on Sri Dakshina Murthy , Written by Sri Adi Sankaracharya).

(1) Are we puppets in the hands of Destiny? Is everything Predecided by Almighty (Paramatma)?

Ans: No. Almighty neither creates avenues for our actions nor instigates us to act (Gita V:14). It is our nature that decides our destiny. Almighty even do not give the results of our actions. The law of nature (Prakriti) and our nature (Svabhava) decide what we are and what we will act upon.

(2) Who provides the platforms for activities (Karma)?

Ans: It is the 'effect' of qualities that the individual is associated with, that 'causes' the platform for activities (Gita XIII:22). Prakriti is the source for qualities and creator of avenues. It creates avenues that suit the qualities of the individual (Gita III:21).

(3) What is the result of wrong and virtuous deeds? Whether one gets Sin from wrong deeds?

Ans: Wrong actions add ignorance and delusion. In turn, ignorance brings sorrow. Virtuous deeds increase intellect. Almighty neither imposes Sin nor Merit on individuals (Gita V:15).

(4) What is Sin?

Ans: Consolidation of ignorance is Sin. Ignorance word used here is not indicating a lack of knowledge, rather it is referring to ignoring the Divine guidance that everyone receives while doing any activity. It is referring to activities taken up against Divine guidance (Gita X:34). The pleasures and pains associated with such actions are to be borne by the individual as per the Law of Karma (Gita XIII:22)

(5) Can the Law of Karma be escaped by any individual?

Ans: Not possible until ignorance and delusion are washed away.

However, if the individual lit the fire of wisdom in his heart, then it can char the bonds of previous Karma irrespective of the degree of sin committed (IV:19,36,37). When ego ('I'ness) is dissolved Law of Karma can't catch up any more.

(6) What is that wisdom that can pyrolyze the previous Karma and Keep the Individuals away from the Law of Karma?

Ans: The wisdom of Karma Yoga involves being insensitive to the results of actions yet executing the responsibilities with full dedication. It can liberate from the Law of Karma (Gita IV:14,15). Wisdom of Karma Yoga also involves raising to a level where we are not biased by previous attachments. Once anyone reaches such a level, his previous Sins or bondage of Karma will vanish (Gita IV:23)

(7) How to acquire the Wisdom of Karma Yoga?

Ans: One should Know what is the Righteous way of executing the activity, and what is forbidden acts as per Dharma (Vedic and Upanishadic rules). One should also know the perils of renouncing the action. Till these things are known one can't come out of the bondage of Karma (Gita IV:17).

(8) How to execute the responsibilities? What is the outcome of executing the duties with dedication, and a with the impartial mind?

Ans: Keep the senses under the control of the mind. Don't focus on the end result (Gita III:7). Don't allow the end result to constrain your mind. Learn to treat both success and failure with equal seriousness (Gita II:48,49). Think that, the result is decided by the Almighty. You are nominated as his tool or front face to physically accomplish it (Gita XI:34). One has to nurture the art of executing the tasks with skill. The Skill of executing tasks is the Karma Yoga (Gita II:50,51). It will liberate the individual from all Prakritic constraints.

(9) What Kind of work that I need to choose to connect well to Karma Yoga?

Ans: Choose the work that suits your nature. Something that you can effortlessly execute and are passionate about. Something that you can spontaneously do and show a spontaneous inclination to improve further. Then 'work' becomes 'no work'. Choose such work which spontaneously pulls you to work full time where you don't have any feeling of 'no work' (Gita IV:18).

(10) What if I deviate from the above laws of Karma Yoga?

Ans: It leads to frustration, struggle, and unrest. They increase proportionate to the degree of deviation.

(11) What is the most sacred thing in this world? What is the result of having it?

Ans: Wisdom of Karma yoga is the most sacred thing in this world. One who acquires it realises the Atman (Self-realisation) (Gita IV:23,3338).

(12) How will the 'Self Realisation' change the individual?

Ans: The individual who acquires wisdom realises that his body which is acting is only a tool for the one who is dwelling inside it (Atman) (Gita XIII:3).

(13) What is the body made up of? Who made is ?

Ans: The body is made up of 24 attributes of Prakriti. They are intellect (Buddhi), ego, mind (Manah), five senses of cognition namely hearing, touching, seeing, tasting and smelling, five senses of action namely speaking, grasping, moving, excreting, procreating, five subtle elements namely sound, touch, form, taste and smell, five gross elements namely space, wind, fire, water and earth. Excluding intellect, it is made up of 22 attributes. Intellect is the 23rd attribute which is made up of three primitive energies of Prakriti namely Satva (righteousness and compassion), Rajas (Drive for action with an urge to gain something) and Tama (Untruthful, Lazy, Lack of vigour) (Ref: Sankhya Karika of Isvara Krishna & Gita XIII:6,7). The last one among the 24 attributes is Mahat or the intuition that got induced in Prakriti due to its proximity with Paramatma. Prakriti made this body as a dwelling to Atman.

(14) Who is Prakriti ? What are her attributes?

Ans: Prakriti is the mother nature. She is the conscious force created by Paramatma (Creator) for the sake of the elevation of individual souls. It is the one from which the visible and invisible universe is springing out at the beginning of the creation and sliding back at the end (Gita VIII:18). It has both manifest (lower Prakriti) and unmanifest facets

32

(higher Prakriti). At the end of the creation unmanifest facet takes over the manifest facet of Prakriti (Gita VIII: 18). Paramatma seeds individual souls in Prakriti at the beginning of creation (Gita IX:7, XIV:3,4).

(15) Who is Almighty or Paramatma? What are his attributes?

Ans: Paramatma is a Special (Visesha) Soul who was never touched by time, afflicted by pain, bound by results of action (Patanjali Yoga Sutras: I:24). He is the one with the unsurpassed seed of Omniscience. He is manifested as 'OM' and He is 'OM' (PSY: I:25,26, Kathopanishad V:15).

He is above all qualities (Gita XIII.32). He is above visible and invisible, perishable and imperishable (Gita VIII:20, XIII:13, XV:17,18). He is omnipresent, holding the visible, and invisible worlds. Paramatma is so subtle to comprehend with physical tools of the body (Gita XIII:16). He is never born yet living in all entities (Yajurveda: Purusha Sukta). He encompasses everything as one and is never divided. He is the creator, sustainer and the one who merges everything into his fold at the end of the cycle of manifestation (Gita XIII:17).

(16) Where does Paramatma live?

Ans: The abode of Paramatma (God) is above the manifested and un-manifested realms.

It is imperishable and timeless, which can't be visualised through the senses. It is called Brahma Loka or Aksharadham (Gita VIII:16). It is the abode, where once the soul reaches, it gets rid of the cycle of birth and death (Gita VIII:21). It is the abode which is the source of light to all other lights (Kathopanishad Verse 15). However, Paramatma also lives in our hearts (Gita XIII:23,32, Gita XVIII:61).

(17) What is Soul (Jeevatma)?

Ans: It is the conscious force which is experiencing joy and sorrows (Gita XIII:20,21).

(18) What are the attributes of Jeevatma?

Ans: It is the imperishable & eternal entity present in the body. The senses are superior to the body. Mind is superior to senses. Intellect is superior to Mind. One which is superior to intellect is the soul (Gita III:42). Soul does not perish at death (Gita II:20,22).

(19) How to recognise or self-realise the Jeevatma?

Ans: Ignorance born out of the surrender of the mind to senses is shielding the Jeevatma. (Gita III:40,41). One has to tame senses, control the mind, and condition the intellect to behold the Jeevatma (Gita III:41,42).

In the process of doing so, individual acquires the intellect required to burn the Karmic attachments (the feeling of "I" as the doer and the resultant bondage) (Gita IV: 37, 38). Then the individual can understand that the soul is the life force of the body.

(20) Where does Jeevatma (soul) and Paramatma live in the body?

Ans: Jeevatma is present everywhere in the body (Gita III:33). Jeevatma is also referred to as Purusha in Bhagavad Gita (Gita III:33). Paramatma is seated in the heart of the individual's body (Gita: XIII:23). He is above Purusha.

(21) What the world is made up of?

Ans: It is made up of a Trinity called Jeevatma (also called Purusha), Prakriti (Nature or Sakti or Mother Goddess) and Paramatma (Visesha Purusha)

(22) Does the Almighty (Paramatma) has shape and form?

Ans: Prakriti and Paramatma are inseparable. Prakriti is manifested facet of Paramatma. Prakriti has both form and formless facets. Paramatma is above form and formless concepts. At the same time, Paramatma is everything that is visible and invisible. He is Sacred OM (Gita VIII:13).

Thus, Almighty assumes both form and formless dimensions. He is above these two facets as well (Gita XIII:15, (Brihadaranyaka Upanishad: 2.3.1). When he manifests, he manifests like a thousand Suns shining in the sky. He looks gracious and pleasant to those who are righteous. For the wicked, he looks fierce (Gita XI.12, 27). In his Viswaroopa sandarshana (Display of Cosmic form that encompasses the entire universe) Almighty has shown his innumerable forms indicating he owns every form (Gita: XI)

(23) Which is a better way of beholding Almighty? With form or without form?

Ans: Almighty in a defined form is called Vigraha (Idol). As per Amarakosam, the most authentic Sanskrit book, Vigraha (Viseshena atmana gruhyataha iti vigrahaha) means the form that our mind can absorb the attributes of Paramatma in a lucid and effective manner. Yoga and Meditation prefer a form or a sacred memory to focus the mind and withdraw it from worldly distractions (Patanjali Yoga Sutras: Chapter II & IV).

(24) Why can't I see Atman or Almighty?

Ans: As long as there is body consciousness, it is not possible to behold the soul. At a given time one can have either body consciousness or consciousness of soul but not both at the same time (Patanjali Yoga Sutras: Chapter IV:20). Detachment from senses is the most essential step to behold Almighty (Gita VI: 35,36).

(25) What is Yoga? How to practice yoga?

Ans: It is the ability to control the dynamic activity (Vritti) of the mind and tune it with the Soul (Gita VI:26, Patanjali Yoga Sutras: I/1). To Practice Yoga, one has to know why and where the mind is wandering, and how to arrest it.

(26) How to control the mind (Gita VI:34)?

Ans: The first step in controlling the mind is to understand the vrittis (dynamics) of the mind. They are memory, imagination, sleep, dwelling in sense perception or dwelling in error (Patanjali Yoga Sutras: I:6). By practising dispassion towards sensual pleasures mind can be controlled (Patanjali Yoga Sutras: I:15,16).

(27) What else needs to be done to still the mind? What is the best way to have a peaceful mind?

Ans: One needs to cultivate friendship not enviousness with those who are happy, be compassionate towards those in distress, and practice composure and calmness towards those who are non-virtuous. This eases the mind and sharpens its focus (Patanjali Yoga Sutras: I: 33).

Best Way to have Peaceful Mind is to Offer the Fruits of Actions at the Feet of Almighty (GitaXII:12)

(28) Is it wrong to derive pleasure from the senses?

Ans: No. It is not wrong as long as the path of Dharma (righteousness) is not deviated (Gita VII:11).

(29) Whether overindulgence and experiencing sensual pleasures is the best way to satisfy the senses so that the mind will not seek more?

Ans: Senses are like fire, and desires are like fuel. Uncontrolled desires derail the course of the journey of life. They will never let the mind work at its full capacity. People with desires under control can show discretion towards good and bad (Gita II:67). Indulging in sensual pleasures can never satisfy senses. Moreover, they start seeking more.

(30) Why a person is not able to focus, and not able to take a firm decision? Why the mind is fickle? (Gita VI:34)

Ans: It becomes fickle either because the person is not having sufficient know-how of the situation or because the person has not overpowered the senses completely. Another possibility is, he is not detached from the fruits of actions (Gita II:68)

(31) Are there any other methods to prune the senses and focus the mind on the right things?

Ans: Simple and effective way is to seek the company of people who are progressing in the path of Satvik life (life of detachment, devotion & surrender) (Gita X: 8,9). When we are in the right company, the spiritual journey will get accelerated with the blessing of the almighty. He will light the lamp of wisdom in the heart of people who gather to discuss pious things (Gita X:9,10,11).

(32) Till what extent the senses will keep troubling a spiritual seeker?

Ans: Till the seeker sees and beholds the Divinity or Paramatma, senses will keep troubling (Gita II:59). Spiritual journey is like a snake and ladder game. Till the last leap the struggle with the senses especially with the basic instincts should be continued with the utmost caution (Gita III:39).

(33) How to protect ourselves from the pull of senses?

Ans: Withdrawing from the places and things that will tempt the senses and protecting the thoughts under the shield of Dharma (like a tortoise withdraws itself into the shield when it feels there is a threat. (Gita II: 58)

(34) Who are our true friends and true enemies?

Ans: The mind which surrendered to the senses is the real enemy, and the mind which overpowered the senses is the true friend (Gita VI:5)

(35) Is it right to try to behold the infinite God in the form of an Idol or picture or he is to be worshipped as a formless God (Gita XII:1)?

Ans: 12th Chapter of the Bhagavad Gita opens up with this question from Arjuna. Lord Krishna replies in simple terms that, it is not important whether someone is worshipping a formless God or with a defined form. What is important is devotion & steadfast faith. He goes on to say that, as long as the body consciousness prevails, firmly fixing the mind on a formless God is very difficult (Gita XII:5). To have unwavering devotion, focusing on the graceful form of Almighty that was experienced by the seers is essential (Refer Chapter I of Patanjali Yoga Sutras).

God's forms are sometimes represented as Vigraha (Idol). As per Amarakosam, the most authentic Sanskrit book, Vigraha (Viseshena atmana gruhyataha iti vigrahaha) means it is the form that mind can easily focus upon and grasp. Vigraha (Idol) is the gateway to enter into the realm of Divinity. The need for Vigraha is further elaborated below.

It is difficult to control the mind and the feeling of "I" ness (Ahamkara). It needs sustained practice to do so (Gita VI:35). As long as one has body consciousness or "I" ness, it needs a tool to focus its mind on the attributes of God, otherwise like the air; "I" spreads its activities towards recollecting past or imagining future or sliding into the sleep (Gita VI: 34, Patanjali Yoga Sutras I: 5-10). Fixing the mind on the attributes or any of the infinite shapes of God with devotion for long period, cultivating dispassion on other things ensures weakened "I" ness, thereby letting the doors open for the blissful experience of true self-consciousness (Gita VI:26, (Patanjali Yoga Sutras I: 10-15). Observe where the mind is wandering and try to fix on the thought of the moment, and don't allow to wander further (Gita VI:26). Once this state is reached the seeker experiences the bliss of Jeevatma interacting directly with Paramatma (Gita VI:27,28). Till this state is reached, one has to take the assistance of any of the shapes or attributes of Paramatma.

Trying to behold the infinite in a manner comprehendible to the human mind is the first step in the course of Yoga. Paramatma being infinite his attributes are present and pervade the Idol as well. It can shower blessings on the devotee as much as the infinite Paramatma can. (Gita VII: 21). With devotion even a mountain, tree, river or any other thing can be worshipped as Paramatma is present and pervades everything (Gita

X:42). Refer to the story of Prahlada where Almighty appeared from a pillar.

(36) How to surrender to God?

Ans: Shed the ego, the "I" ness. Shedding the ego needs a dedicated effort. It includes overpowering senses, mind and conditioning the intellect to see everything and everywhere God and God alone (Gita VI:29). Do every act as a service to God. Practice offering the fruits of your actions to God. This is the best way of surrender (Gita XII: 12).

(37) Why there are multiple forms of God?

Ans: God descended many times for the sake of saving the virtuous and punishing the wicked. Each time he took a form matching the occasion. (Gita IV:8). This led to many forms for God.

(38) Is it possible to invoke God in Plants, Trees, Mountains, Rivers, animals etc?

Ans: Yes. By saying no to it, we only question the omnipresence of the Almighty. God himself told that "everything in this visible and invisible world is pervaded and penetrated by me. Everything is in me (Gita X.42)". However, there are certain entities where divinity can be effortlessly comprehended by the human mind. Like Peepal tree among trees, Himalayans among mountains, Sage Narada among heavenly beings, Ganges among rivers, Oceans among water bodies, Kamadhenu, Iravata etc among animals & Vasuki among the Snakes (Gita X. 24-32). Any of these manifestations of the Almighty can be used to hook our minds to the vastness of the Almighty.

(39) Which is the best Salutation, the salutations offered to Nature or Salutations to the one who created it/God?

Ans: By differentiating between nature and the creator, the omnipresence of the Creator is defeated. The human mind can't comprehend or conceive the vastness, and subtleness of the creator (Gita II: 25). However, the human mind can comprehend the attributes of nature. The attributes of nature are tools created by God to reach his abode. By beholding any of the attributes of the Prakriti like the mightiness of oceans, tallness of mountains, mighty flow of rivers, and lifesaving or enriching qualities of specific trees; one can weaken the ego and rise above the body consciousness. Salutations offered with sacred hearts in a Satvik manner to any visible or invisible entity reach God . This is because there is nothing different from God (Gita XIII: 30,31). The seventh Chapter of Yajurveda is called "Namaka and Chamaka Prasna". This chapter hails Lord Siva as various manifestations of nature. Salutations offered to Prakritic manifestations with Satvik thoughts are as good as salutations to the invisible life force behind the visible Prakriti.

However, Salutations offered with violent thoughts, and deeds (offerings made by troubling own body or other living beings) are the ignorant way of Salutation.

(40) What if we don't care for God?

Ans: God will never punish those who don't care about him, nor promote those who praise him. No one is his friend or foe (Gita IX:29). Law of Karma will dictate the fate of every individual. Those who don't care for God also can move up the ladder and reach Divine realms provided he or she nurtures the Satvik qualities (quality of compassion, truthfulness, walking the talk etc-.). God is a companion and observer of the journey of each soul (Gita XIII:23). However, those who surrender their ego & 'I' ness can effortlessly cross the ocean of 'Law or Karma' as it can't catch God and those who live in his companionship (Gita XIII:34).

(41) What if there is no God and Soul?

Ans: This question falls under the Charvaka School of Indian Philosophy. However, even if the question is valid, still the path of the Dharma/righteousness pronounced in the sacred texts will ensure a purposeful life and peaceful society (Gita II:26). It brings uniformity in human values, and ensures the continuity of human thought and evolution. However, Bhagavad Gita condemns such atheistic thinking. Such thinking is narrow-minded thinking. It may lead to moral degradation in society (Gita XVI:9,12).

(42) What is the use of Praying to God?

Ans: When sought, he washes off Karmic bondage. He will ensure quick relief from the sufferings (Gita IX:31). He will take care of the well-being (Gita IX: 22).

(43) Whether anyone becomes superior by birth?

Ans: Among human beings, no one is superior or inferior by birth. If anyone thinks in this way based on his race, colour etc. it is his ignorance. It is the demonic quality which needs to be shed (Gita XVI: 15).

However, taking birth into a family which is pious, and prosperous is an indication of righteous acts in the past life. Such an opportunity is bestowed on the seeker so that, he can continue his spiritual journey smoothly. A few seekers get the opportunity of taking birth into a family of Yogis having Divine wisdom and dispassion towards materialistic assets. Such a birth is a rare chance given to selected souls which have matured in their spiritual journey yet are still short of eligibility for complete liberation at the time of leaving the body in the previous life. (Gita VI: 41,42).

(44) What is birth?

Ans: The soul which is in the unmanifest form taking the manifested form & getting the required tools (intellect) to feel the consciousness of Paramatma (Super soul) is birth (Gita II:28, XIII:23). An otherwise dormant Soul regains consciousness due to the celestial touch of Paramatma.

(45) What is death?

Ans: Paramatma leaving the company of Jeevatma thereby making the latter lose consciousness of the body is Death. The moment Paramatma withdraws from the body, Jeevatma forgoes the ability to use some of the tools of Prakriti like intellect and consciousness (Gita XIII:2,3). It is like iron losing its magnet like nature when moved away from the source magnet. Thus, Jeevatma goes into a dormant state. This is death.

(46) Where does the soul travel and stay during an unmanifest state?

Ans: The soul which nurtured (the individual who nurtured) the right-eous path and used the given opportunity to elevate self in the mani-fested state (when present in the earthly world with the body), travels in the path which is glowing by Divine light. It is like part of the earth orienting itself towards more Sunrays during solstice followed by six months of proximity to the Sun (Gita VIII:24). There in the realms of light and comfort, the Soul (called 'Prayata' in Gita) basks in the bliss of Paramatma. After staying there for a long time, the Soul takes the man-ifested form again. This time the avenue (the family in which it takes birth) it chooses, will be better than the previous birth enabling it to progress further in the path of Paramatma (Gita VIII:24).

Souls which left their body after wasting the opportunities given in life leaves the body in a state of delusion. They travel away or skids away from the Paramatma similar to the areas of the earth oriented away from the Sun when the Sun is shining more on the other part of the earth's hemisphere. After sliding down to such realms that were having ob-scured light the soul realises the wasted opportunities. Like the moon brights up the night skies, the spark of Soul then brightens up its path and returns to the manifested form to continue the effort of elevating itself (Gita VIII:25).

(47) What does one (Soul) carry during death?

Ans: The soul carries the essence of qualities the individual has nurtured. It is like the wind carrying the fragrance of the flowers leaving the flowers behind, the soul carries the qualities of the individual (Gita XV:8, XVIII:47)

(48) When can the Soul jump out of the cycle of birth and death (Gita VIII: 13,16)?

Ans: If one can chant the Sacred Sound 'OM' while leaving the body, then his or her soul will reach the realm of Paramatma (Gita IIX: 13,16). However out of thousands of seekers, one can achieve these feet (Gita VII:3). Those who fail to do so yet aspired for it and practiced the path of Dharma, will travel in the path lit by Divine light, reach heavenly realms which are free from hunger, thirst, disease, calamities, old age etc. After staying there for a long time, they will turn back to the earthly world and take birth into a pious family. (Gita VI:41)

(49) Out of many realms that are present in the path of Brahma loka (the abode of Paramatma), which realm the Soul reaches after leaving the body?

Ans: The final thought before leaving the body drives the soul towards the realm which it deserves to reach (Gita VIII:6). The final thought made before leaving the body is the aggregate of the thoughts individual nurtured during his lifetime. If the aggregate of the thoughts is pious like compassion, non-violence, and truthful then the soul reaches the realms which are full of comfort (Heavens) (Gita XIV:14). If the aggregate of the thoughts is average between the good and bad the soul immediately takes birth on the earth (Gita XIV:15). If the aggregate of the thoughts is full of deceit, untruthful, violent, narrow-minded, foolish & wild then the Soul reaches the realms of darkness. After completing its stay there, it returns to the earthly realm but takes a life which is lower than the life it got in the previous birth in terms of physical form (maybe animals if nurtured only animal instincts), or as humans but into such circumstances which on an aggregate takes the individual towards the foolish and wild thoughts. (Gita XIV: 15).

(50) Are there any other things that influence the birth and death cycle other than good and bad deeds one has done in his life?

Ans: If one dies while discharging his duty (like a Soldier/King dying on the battlefield) he reaches the heavenly abodes of light and comfort (Gita II: 32). His readiness to sacrifice life for the duty (Karma Yoga) washes off all his Karmic bonds. On the other hand, if one realises and repents the mistakes and takes refuge at the feet of Paramatma he will come out of the 'Law of Karma' or from the clutches of his sins (Gita XVIII:66).

(51) Are there any such activities of the living people, that can influence the elevation of the soul of their forefathers?

Ans: The acts done in the earthly realms bring quick results (Gita IV:12). One can do the penances, prayers, and good deeds and offer the resultant Karma to the forefathers who can receive it (Gita IX: 25) (Study this sloka in the context of Gita IX: 24, 26 and 27 to understand better that the performer of the good deeds/Yagna can decide on who should be the receiver of the results of these good deeds). The performer of the good deeds can own it for himself, offer to forefathers, or offer it to the Paramatma. It is recommended not to own the results of good deeds.

This is because even the good deeds also hold the one from moving up the ladder of elevation as he has to enjoy the fruits of his good deeds and for this, he has to stay in the cycle of birth and death (Gita IX: 28)

(52) How long Jeevatma will be shuttling between birth and death?

Ans: Till Jeevatma realises that the Paramatma is present in everybody, and stop troubling, envying and hating others (thereby stops to hate Paramatma) (Gita XVI: 21,22, V:7). Till the individual starts working with the feeling of I am not the doer he will keep shuttling (Gita III:27). The day individual experiences the omnipresence of Paramatma he can break the chain of birth and death.

(53) Whether people of different schools of religious thoughts reach different realms after death?

Ans: There are many realms of Divinity. Soul elevates to such a Divine realm for which one has longed - for during his life (Gita VII:15,16). However, all such souls will return to the earthly realm after a long blissful stay in the chosen Divine realm. However, those spiritual seekers who believed that "all the spiritual forms are the same, and any Satvik prayer offered to any Divine form is reaching the same Almighty" will reach a realm from where there is no need to return to earthly realms again (Gita VIII:5,8). Such Spiritual seekers understood the oneness of the Almighty and thus reach the ultimate realm. This is irrespective of the religious school he practiced. It takes wisdom accumulated over many births to behold such a level of all-pervasiveness of the Almighty (Gita VII:18,19).

(54) Whether changing my religious thought/ school/affiliation will help me get my soul elevated?

Ans: No, change your heart, not the religious school. All will reach the same abode based on how much refinement the heart had (Gita V.5). One should understand, it is the one supreme Lord who is worshipped by seekers of various denominations, it is the same Law of nature that is giving fruits of actions to seekers of all denominations or even to those who are not worshipping any God yet doing their duties (Chapter VII:11,12,21). Seekers who sought the truth and yearned for it will reach the same abode of truth and bliss (Gita IV:10).

(55) Shall I quit my duty, if as part of duty, war is to be waged or violence is to be resorted to so that I can escape the Sin of violence? (This is the main theme of the question raised by Arjuna in Bhagavad Gita in chapter I and II)

Ans: Acts done as part of duty (a soldier in war or one who hangs a proven accused to death) will not result in sin as long as he is doing it as his duty. It will not bring sin as long as it is done without hatred or prejudice (Gita. III:35). In fact, running away from duty with such excuses will bring frustration and sin. It is the feeling (Noble feelings of love towards humanity, righteousness or wicked feeling of hatred, determination to uphold the order) that is present in mind while executing the action, that makes a person a noble person or sinner, not the action itself.

(56) How to execute the responsibilities of Duty or a given activity? What is the outcome of executing the duties with dedication, and with an impartial mind?

Ans: Execute the duty as if it is a prayer to God. Execute it as if the task is given to you by God himself. Leave the fruits to God (Gita II: 48,49). Don't think I am the doer, think that, the task is already executed by Almighty (in the Divine realms through his Divine action). You are nominated as his tool or front face to physically accomplish it (Gita XI:34). One has to nurture the art of executing the tasks with skill. The Skill of executing tasks is the Karma Yoga or a prayer offered to Lord through action (Gita II:50,51). One need not do any more austerities if he imbibes the true essence of Karma Yoga. He will be freed from the bondage of the cycle of life and death. It is to be understood that duties are not confined to professional life alone, they encompass the personal life and its responsibilities as well.

(57) What are the consequences of Tamasik acts (acts of Laziness, violence)? What are its consequences?

Ans: They pile up ignorance. Ignorance is Sin (V:15). It ensures that the Soul is tied to the cycle of birth and death (Gita XVI:20). Tamasik acts with the feeling of 'I' am the doer will pull the Soul towards the lower realms where the problem of hunger and the disease is more. It may sometimes lead to taking birth as an animal which suits the temperament that was nurtured in his life (Gita XIII:22).

(58) Are the prayers answered?

Ans: Those who are devotees of God will never perish. God will take care of their well-being (Gita IX:22). God himself told to his devotees to proclaim it to all. He will ensure that the promise given by his devotees to those in suffering that, "*by seeking the refuge at the feet of Almighty, you will never perish*", will never go waste (Gita IX:31). Not only the day-to-day issues, even the most complex issues like the old age, death can also be overcome when we seek refuge at the feet of Almighty (Gita VII:29). Rest assured that, every prayer will be answered

(59) Whom Shall I worship? Lord Siva, Vishnu, Krishna, Ganesha?

Ans: There is no multiplicity of Godhood (Gita X: 42, XI: 5,7,15). Each form of Godhood is a manifestation of one or other attributes of Infinite and limitless Paramatma. Lord Siva is to be invoked by those who wish to follow the path of Yoga, Lord Vishnu or Krishna is to be invoked by those who wish to follow the path of Devotion, Lord Ganesha is to be invoked by those who wish to follow the path of discriminative contemplation to overcome the hurdles of the spiritual journey. So are various other forms of Godhood. Whomever the devotee invokes with devotion, the answer comes from the same Maheswara who is seated in the heart of the devotee (Gita VII:21).

(60) What if I follow the lifestyle prescribed in this book (the sacred texts) or don't follow it?

Ans: If you follow, peace in both material and spiritual realms is assured. If you don't follow these guidelines yet follow a path of truth, non-violence and compassion towards all, then it is as good as following the message of sacred texts. If anyone lives a life of free will guided by basic instincts of senses then it is certain that he or she will never find peace in this world, nor find a place in the eternal world (Gita XVI: 23,24).

(61) Is our birth in this life predecided? Is it possible to change our future course?

Ans: Yes, it is pre-decided by Prakriti who is governing the universe based on the Law of Karma (Gita IV: 5, Gita VI;43,44). She has allotted us the birth that we have taken based on the total of qualities that we nurtured in our previous births and acts that were done in our previous births. It is difficult to tame or trim the qualities nurtured over many births (Gita VI:34). The actions that we indulge in now are the results of thoughts we nurtured previously. The thoughts we nurture now are the results of the qualities that we carry. The results of actions and thus the kind of life that we live are the accumulated dues that that we are receiving from the Prakriti.

However, it can be refined by the practice of Sankhya Yoga (Gita II:39). Sankhya Yoga is a Yoga of Wisdom. It can burn the Karmic bonds (Gita XIV:23,36,37). Karmic bonds can also be broken with Karma yoga (Gita XIV:20-23). It involves doing the duty as a service to God, doing the duty without ego or fear and offering the results of the work at the feet of the Almighty (Gita XIV:20-23).

It is to be noted that, Maheswara controls the Prakriti (Gita IX:8-10). Based on our eagerness to shed the ego and earnest request to uplift from ignorance, the Almighty can trigger wisdom in our minds , can wash away the ignorance of past actions (sins) or the Karmic chains (Gita XVIII:66). Thus, we can change our destiny by shedding ego, and tuning ourselves with the Almighty.

(62) What is the essence of the Bhagavad Gita and Upanishads?

Ans: Almighty is one, whatever the form you pray, the same Almighty will shower the blessing (Gita IX:23). **Shedding the ego, and utmost faith in the Almighty are the two basic messages of Bhagavad Gita.** Once these two are imbibed, Divinity within will manifest. Even if in past one has committed many sins, the moment these qualities are imbibed he will be liberated from the effects of past actions **Becoming a good human being is the first essential step to succeed in material and spiritual life** (Gita IX:22,30,31).

(63) **Is God dictating every moment of our life?** What are the Riddles in Bhagavad Gita regarding this question?

Ans: This question is answered in question (1) itself in this chapter. However, a section of scholars emphasise that everything is predecided by God, we are mere objects in his play. They quote Gita XI:33, where Lord Krishna has told to Arjuna that *"Kaurava warriors were already killed by me, you just become a mere actor to act the play"*. Is this not indicating we are mere puppets in play? To answer this, one should read Gita XI:32 where Lord Krishna told that, he is the 'Time (Kala)" that consumes everything. He told in XI:32 that, even if you don't kill them, they will not survive. In XI:29, it is indicated that it is the Kaurava warriors who are running into the mouth of death like the moths running into a blazing fire. This infers again that it is the Svabhava (nature) of the people which decides their fate. The nature and qualities that Kauravas nurtured were self-destructive. They churned the fire of destruction through their Svabhava and thus invoked Prakriti to provide a suitable avenue for the same (Gita V:14).

Thus, their destruction was certain which is the result of their own actions. At the same time what is not certain is Arjuna Killing them. Lord Krishna has not told to Arjuna that, "I decided that, you shall kill them in war". Lord Krishna told us that, even if Arjuna leaves Kauravas, their death is certain (Gita XI:32). In other slokas also Lord Krishna told to Arjuna to wage the war as it is his duty to fight for the right cause. Lord Krishna told to Arjuna 'if you die during discharging duty, your sacrifice of the life for right cause will bestow you heaven and in case you win you can enjoy the Kingdom' (Gita II:37). This indicates that Arjuna is free to choose his course. He is not a puppet. The death of Kauravas is certain which is due to the destructive nature that they nurtured. Waging war by Arjuna and winning it is not decided by Almighty. It is Arjuna who has to take a call based on his own Svabhava (nature).

One more Sloka in Bhagavad Gita with which many get confused is Gita III:33 which says that even the "Gnani" (one with Knowledge) is bound by Prakriti and he can't control his acts under the pull of Prakriti. When it is read in combination with Gita III:27 it infers that, those who feel "I" am the doer are in delusion. It is the Prakriti that is deciding the acts and avenues for action.

Thus, we are puppets in the hands of Destiny. This is how the proponents of the 'Hand of Destiny' using these slokas.

However, it should be understood that Prakriti referred to in these slokas includes the nature (svabhava) of the individual. It should be read in combination with Gita III:29, which indicates that people of low intellect keep moving in the flow of Gunas (qualities) of Prakriti and get deluded that they are acting, ***whereas the wisemen realises that it is the qualities that they are carrying that are triggering various actions. Thus, they try to stand out from the rest to create their destiny by coming out of previous inclinations.*** Thus, as long as one doesn't make a conscious effort he cannot come out of the spell of Prakriti and its energies. For such people, Prakriti is acting not they. They have become puppets in the hands of qualities that they have sourced from Prakriti.

One should not miss a subtle point here that, finally activity is executed by the energies of Prakriti (Gunas), and the result is decided by the Laws of nature, however, what energies (Gunas) one chooses and in what proportion (Satva, Raja, Tamas) to be deployed for a given action and thus the outcome of the action is in the hands of Individual.

See Gita III:36 where Arjuna asked why are the people being forcefully deployed by Prakriti to involve in various acts that will ultimately make them struggle. Here Lord Krishna replied that (Gita III:37) it is the wrong selection of qualities like lust, and anger by Individuals which brings them under the spell of nature making them puppets in the hands of destiny. However, if you choose the right energies of Prakriti through wisdom, you can come out of this spell of Prakriti and thus from the clutches of acts that may bind you to a wrong destiny (Gita III:41).

Please note that the great scholar of our times Dr Sarvepalli Radha Krishnan also expressed the same opinion that, we are not bound by destiny. We can decide and change the course of the future. These views he expressed in his essay on Vedanta (Ref: Prakpaschima Tatva Sastramu Published by Andhra University). Swamy Ranganatha Nanda who served as head seer of Rama Krishna Mission for a long time also expressed a similar opinion in his commentary on Bhagavad Gita.

(64) Can there be answers to questions that were not expressed or asked?

Ans: Yes, provided we are in communion with the Almighty. Prakritic medium is required as long as we don't establish direct communion with the Almighty. In the final state of absorption when we surrender our ego, the Almighty uses various methods to answer all our questions in silence. The devotee can absorb them completely without using any of the body tools or senses. This is the highest state of devotion. In this state, the role of Prakriti ceases. It is advised to all seekers to try it for the questions that are still lingering in their minds.

Chapter III

The Genesis- Vedic and Bhagavad Gita's View

Prelude: This section brings out an integrated view of the Vedas, Upanishads, and Bhagavad Gita on the origin of the universe and creation. It identifies three eternal entities which act as a cornerstone for the creation. They are Paramatma (Super soul), Prakriti and the Jeevatma (Soul). These three together form the Divine trinity. During the pralaya (dissolution of the universe) Paramatma becomes the final resting place for the Prakriti and Jeevatma. Manifestation and dissolution of the universe is cyclic in nature. Every Jeevatma carries the seed force of Paramatma and the qualities from Prakriti. Thus, Paramatma and Prakriti act like father and mother for the Jeevatma.

The Genesis: Paramatma (Super soul or Purushottama or Maheswara) was the only entity in the beginning as he was beginningless and endless. Paramatma was not bound by time and space. At the feet of Paramatma time ceases to exist. Neither light nor darkness, neither near nor far, neither being nor nonbeing can be felt in it. We offer our salutations to this supreme soul (Rigveda X:121). It is the fountain from which the universe springs up at the beginning of the Kalpa (time scale to measure the age of creation) and slides back (Gita IX:7). It offered timeless ecstasy to souls by devouring all the illusionary (maya in Sanskrit) platforms that made them divert attention from him. It is the golden womb in which all the souls rest at pralaya. They are waiting to manifest again in the next cycle of creation. It is the embodiment of everything that is going to manifest as creation, it has devoured the previous creation and is about to precipitate a new cycle of creation (Gita VIII:18).

Paramatma wished that "I will make worlds out of my being". He made different worlds. Then Paramatma thought let me make the administrator (Loka Palaka) for the worlds. As Paramatma hatched the thought of administrator, the mouth of the Purusha broke forth humming the sound OM, thus representing its creator i.e., Paramatma. From the mouth, the fire is born. Then the nostrils of the Purusha broke forth, through the nostrils the breath and thus the air was born. From the air the life force emanated, then the eyes broke forth, and from the eyes sight and of the sight Sun was born. The ears broke forth and from the ears hearing and of the hearing all the quarters of space were born. The skin broke forth and from the skin hairs, herbs of healing and all trees and plants were born. The heart broke forth and from the heart Mind (Manah) and of mind the moon was born. The organ broke forth and from the organ seed and of seed the waters were born. Thus administrator (Prajapati) has emerged out of the will of Paramatma to administer the universe.

Prajapati created Gods (Gita III-10), and they fall into his great ocean of space. Gods are celestial beings and the inhabitants of heaven. Hunger and thirst leapt on celestial beings. They sought the help of Prajapati. He brought forth cow and horse for them. They were not satisfied by these.

They sought more for their habitation. Then Prajapathi meditated deeply on Paramatma (Gita III-10). From his own being, he generated humans in his image (Gita XV-7). He commanded fire to enter the mouth of humans and become his speech. He commanded air to become human's breath and to enter his nostrils. He commanded the Sun to become his sight and enter his eyes, and all quarters of space to become hearing of humans and to enter in ears. He commanded the herbs of healing and plants to become the hair of humans and to enter their skin, commanded the moon to become mind and enter humans. Prajapati commanded death to become humans down the breath and enter the navel. He commanded waters to become seed force and enter the organ of humans.

Prajapathi brooded over habitation for human beings. He contemplated this thought and prayed the Paramatma from which emerged a conscious force called Prakriti which was devoured by Paramatma at the end of the previous cycle of creation (Gita VII-7). It was latently present in the Paramathma along with Jeevatmas that have not completed their ascent to the abode of Liberation or unification with Paramathma in the previous cycle of creation (Gita XIV:3). Prakriti permeated all through the creation performing the act of creating avenues for the survival of creation. Using the five seed elements of earth, water, heat, air and space it spread all through the universe as the gigantic galaxies, mighty oceans, lofty mountains, birds, animals, plants, the seasons etc. It is limitless, creative, and eternal without birth and death, it manifested as many beings and spread entire space with its innumerable forms (Purusha Sukta, Yajurveda). Having engulfed the earth, heavens and waters and all other

59

avenues it permeated humans as the three primitive qualities of Satvik, Rajasik & Tamasik. Using these three primitive energies she tied humans to her order of Law of Karma (Gita XIV:5, XIII:20).

It further crept into the body of human beings as five elements, sensory feelings and crept the Manah (Mind is a loose translation of Manah) as ego (Gita VII:4). As the Prakriti know the past evolutionary status of the individual resting souls it attracted the souls back to its lap by providing them with the physical forms that they are due to get based on their status of evolution (Gita IV-5, IX-8). These individual souls are the same ones which were helplessly merging back into the Paramatma at the end of the creation while during the manifested stage undergoing repeated births and deaths (Gita VIII-18,20).

Thus, the human body became an abode for Jeevatma which experiences the pleasures and pains using the body as a tool (Gita XIII -23). Since it got deeply veiled by the qualities born out of Prakriti, it started to identify itself with the body (Gita XIII:22). It lost itself in devouring and digesting the good, bad and the ugly sprinkled over its mind by the Prakriti (Gita XIII-20). Jeevatma dwells only in Prakriti while unable to recognize the onlooker and original creator that is Paramatma. (Brihadaranyaka Upanishad, Nasadiya Sukta)

Prakriti allowed souls to seek pleasures and pains by indulging in its resources. Thus, it was fully resurrected and formed as a veil between humans and Prajapathi (3rd Canto of Aitareya Brahmana). Prajapathi tried to bring the veil under his control by his sight but stopped short of doing so as humans who were created in his image would then be using only sight to overcome the veil. He thought of controlling the veil by his ears, then he thought humans will then be confined to only listening to overcome the veil. He realized that all these sensory tools which are part of Prakriti can't be made as a tool to break its veil.

He pondered on how I can enter the human beings circumventing the veil, as all organs like mouth, eyes, nostrils, ears, skin, and mind were occupied by Prakriti and its varied manifestations. Where is the seat for me in the human body? Prajapathi thought 'I'' am not ears, 'I' am not eyes, 'I' am not skin, 'I' am not breath, he entered the human's body as a discretion of who am 'I'. He seated himself in the cleft of the body. This cleft is in the heart which is in the form of a lotus situated along the line of the throat to the navel seated below the throat. This is the place of Hridaya (heart, not to confuse with physical heart). In the centre of the lotus-shaped heart, a garland of fire is radiating. In the centre of the garland of fire, there is a spherical opening. In the centre of this opening, the glowing fire of a Jeevatma is present as a spark with the size of the tip of the rice husk. At the tip of this spark, Prajapathi is seated. He is seating there as an onlooker of Jeevatma. He is above Jeevatma (Gita XIII:23). Prakriti is constantly supplying life support essential materials and qualities to the Jeevatma which receives it with innumerable tongues and faces. The soul is throwing back its radiance from the tip to the toe of the body.

Thus, the Lord of the universe (Prajapathi) who is the creator of the Gods and support for the universe found his seat in the soul of the human beings, observing every moment of the soul present in the human body. We offer our prayers to the Lord who is Brahma, who is the Hari, who is Siva. He is Akshara (non-perishable and permanent) and supreme (Mantra Pushpa from Krishna Yajurveda)

Paramatma is above the perishable and imperishable. At his feet, the time ceases. Prajapati having created the humans and their habitations and having created Gods, uttered to Gods and humans that, 'together you live and prosper (Gita III-11). Use prayer (yagna) as a tool to milch all your needs from me, I will be the wish-fulfilling cow to answer all your prayers' (Gita III-10)

Conclusion: Super soul (Paramatma) created the administrator (Prajapati). He carried the vigour of Paramatma (also referred to as Parameswara or Purushottama in various texts). Prakriti has come out from the Paramatma to nourish the Jeevatmas. Prakriti is meant for nurturing the universe. Prajapati carries the latent and invisible vigour of Paramatma whereas the Prakriti carries the nourishing nature of Paramatma. The combination of Prajapati and Prakriti created and sustained the universe, Gods (dwellers of heavens), humans, animals, plants, visible and invisible beings, and nonbeings. In essence, Eswara and Prakriti are inseparable creators. Jeevatmas (Individual souls) were given repeated chances by Prakriti and Eswara to ascend the ladder of consciousness from the body to the soul and then towards the Super soul

(Paramatma). The body of human beings is the abode of not only the Jeevatma but also the Eswara.

In the subsequent chapters, a detailed discussion on the Divine trinity and how various philosophical schools evolved with subtle differences of opinion on the Divine trinity is discussed.

Chapter IV

Sankhya, Vedanta & The Divine Trinity: Multiple Paths with One Goal

Prelude: The consciousness level of the individual is a ladder to peep into the Divine realms. Lesser the body consciousness, the deeper the vision into Divine realms. The depth and the vastness of the divine attributes are beyond the comprehension of individuals (Gita II-25). After rigorous personal efforts to cleanse the body, mind & intellect, the Almighty graces the individual with the Divine wisdom to behold his vastness (Gita X-10,11 & 22nd Anuvaka, Surya Namaskara Prasna of Taittiriya Aranyaka). For those who are seeking the path of realization, yet not mature enough to dissolve the mind and intellect into the soul within, Almighty himself descended and showed the path in the form of the Bhagavad Gita. It can be used as a compass to reach the abode of the Almighty. This section churns various concepts of the Bhagavad Gita on Jeevatma and how it is related to two other aspects of the Hindu trinity that is Paramatma and Prakriti. This section also answers, "why so many subsects of Hinduism exist and what is the underlying unity among various schools of Hindu thought". The gist of Jainism, Buddhism and Sikhism and what is their take on the Divine Trinity is also discussed towards the end of this chapter. The common joining thread of all religious schools evolved in India is brought out towards the end of this chapter.

"Some seekers get enlightenment through Meditation, others through their Inquisitiveness, others through Sankhya Yoga and a few others through Karma Yoga. Others get enlightenment through hearing about the compassionate Almighty and by worshipping him. All these people can swim across the ocean of ignorance and reach my abode (Gita XIII: 25,26)

As per the sacred Indian texts, there exists a Divine trinity. They are

(i) Mother Nature referred to in Indian texts as Prakriti/ Sakti

(ii) Soul within referred to as 'Atman' or 'Jeevatma'

(iii) Super soul or the Almighty referred to as 'Paramatma'.

Two prominent ancient Indian philosophical schools namely Sankhya and Vedanta have had differing views on the relation between the Jeevatma, Paramatma and Prakriti. This has led to the evolution of multiple sects in Hinduism. The following text is an effort to elaborate on the attributes of the Divine trinity from the perspective of these two schools and various sub-sects of Hinduism.

Sankhya School of Thought: It is one of the six orthodox schools of Indian Philosophy. Sage Kapila is identified as one of the earliest pro-pounders of Sankhya. Bhagavad Gita identifies this school as one of the authentic schools to pursue the path of self-realization (Gita V: 4, Gita XIII:25). This school names Paramatma as Purusha who is Pure Wisdom (Suddha Gnana) devoid of material. Paramatma is not constrained by time as time ceases in his realm. As per this school, everything that is seen in the creation has a cause-effect combination. Upadana (Material cause) and Nimitta (Instrument Cause) are intertwined in the cause-and-effect cycle. Creation can't be accidental. The effect lies in the cause in the dormant state before the cause materializes. As per Sankhya school, before the creation, which is the effect, there should be a true cause. Cause carries all the seed qualities of the effect. Thus, the reason for the effect to manifest from the cause should be present in the cause itself. This is called 'Satkaryavada' or 'Karya Purva Astitvavada' (The existence of results of an action before the action is taken up). As per the Yoga sutras of Vyasa, Prakriti is the combination of three primitive qualities or three primitive energies. They are Satvik, Rajasik and Tamasik energies. Prakriti provides the material cause for creation using these three energies. Satvik is Pure, noble, compassionate, non-selfish action-oriented energy. Rajasik energy is action-oriented with selfishness imbibed in action. Tamasik is made up of laziness, depression, violent and foolish

66

aspects. These three prime causes or prime energies also carry the seeds of effects along with them.

In essence, if someone is choosing the quality of 'Satvik' for a cause, its positive effects also will follow. When someone is choosing the quality of 'Tamasik' he can't escape from its negative effects. This is because seeds of effect are inbuilt in the cause. This is the basis of the 'Law of Karma"

Before the start of the creation, Prakriti is present as the 'Mahat' (or Buddhi) in Paramatma. It is the effect that is subtly present in the Cause that is Paramatma. It is called 'Mahat' since it is too vast for the time to constrain it. So, it is beginning and endless (Gita XIII:20). At the start of the creation, Mahat shrunk as one of the three primitive qualities namely 'Satvik qualities' which took predominance over the other two primitive qualities. This triggered a turbulence and ripple effect which kickstarted a series of attributes of Prakriti having different proportions of three primitive energies. They manifested as visible matter and invisible (matter less) entities All the visible and invisible that got manifested were divided into 24 different attributes by Sankhya school. Unlike Paramatma and Mahat, these 24 attributes or facets of Prakriti are constrained by time. Twenty-four attributes as per the Sankhya school are listed below (Gita XIII:6,7, VII:4, XV:9).

• Five prime elements namely earth, water, fire, air and space; five subtle elements having parity with prime elements in that order Viz smell, taste, form, touch, and sound which form ten attributes out of 24 attributes of mother nature (Prakriti). These ten are offered by Prakriti as external energies to the Jeevatmas (beings). Ten more attributes of Prakriti become internal to Jeevatmas. They are

• Five Karmendriyas or five senses of action namely speaking, grasping, moving, excreting, and procreating along with five buddhendriyas or five senses of cognition namely nose or smelling, tongue or tasting, eyes or seeing, sense of touching, ear or hearing constitute the next set of ten attributes offered by Prakriti to Jeevatma.

• Mind (called as Chitta as per Indian texts) or consciousness of an individual which coordinates with the external and internal sources of mother nature constitutes the twenty-first attribute offered by Prakriti to Jeevatma.

• The ego (Ahamkara) or self-identity of individual forms the 22nd attribute, while the Intellect of an individual evolved out of stirring of senses with the mind forming the 23rd attribute. Along with these 23 attributes, the 'Mahat which is the highest and most subtle form of Prakriti (the intuition of Prakriti) makes the twenty-fourth attribute of the Prakriti. All these 24 attributes together make mother nature which is widely referred to as 'Prakriti/Sakti' in the Hindu texts

Prakriti is the perceivable manifestation. Paramatma is above Prakriti and subtler than Prakriti (Gita VII:5). He is different from visible and invisible. Prakriti works under the supervision of Paramatma (Gita IX:10). Most debated question of whether God has shape or not was simply answered by Sankhya. Paramatma doesn't have any shape or expressible form whereas the Prakriti has the form and shape. Since Paramatma doesn't have any shape, he is indicated by Linga. 'Amarakosam' the authentic dictionary for root words of Sanskrit, says that the root sound of 'Linga' represents "Lingyate Gyayate Aneneti Lingam", meaning it represents and reveals something which can't be represented in any form. It is a symbolic form to remind the existence of something, which can't be depicted, whereas the Prakriti is represented as Goddess in her full splendid attire as she has the quality of manifesting in the perceivable form.

Siva Linga depicts 'Sadhya' (Anumana Pramana) about the existence of Paramatma who can't be comprehended or depicted completely. Hence indicated by a symbol that is Linga. Prakriti refers to the conscious life force that can be experienced. Please refer to Pratyaksha Pramana and Anumana Pramana proposed by Nyaya and Vaiseshika School (Refer to Chapter I for more details)

Every Hindu temple is a standing testimony to show how Sankhya thought got imbibed into the Hindu thought process. Prakriti takes the form as per the will of Paramatma (Prajapati). When the Paramatma wished to uphold the universe as Viswanatha (the Lord of the Universe), Prakriti assumed the form of Annapurna (one who nourishes the universe) and Visalakshi (one with the omnipresent eye). This is what we worship at Varanasi. When Paramatma wished to impart wisdom as Dakshina Murthy, Prakriti assumed the form of Gnana Prasunamba one who dispels ignorance and kindles wisdom. This is what we see at Sri Kalahasti temple. When the Paramatma wished to take the form of Venkateswara (Sanskrit meaning 'one who drives away the difficulties'), Prakriti assumed the form of Goddess Lakshmi one who bestows wealth. This is what we worship at Tirupati. When Paramatma wished to dissolve the creation as Mahakala, Prakriti has taken the form of Mahakali. This is what we worship at Ujjain. Thus, the Purusha and Prakriti are inseparable roots of creation (Gita XIII:20). As per the Bhagavad Gita Paramatma is to be identified as the father of creation and Prakriti as the mother of creation (Gita XIV: 3,4).

Paramatma is the seed-giving Father and Prakriti is the nourishing mother for the Jeevatmas. Prakriti binds the Jeevatmas to the body with three primitive qualities that are Satvik, Rajasik and Tamasik (Gita XIV:4,5).

Jeevatma was part of Paramatma which has come under the contact of Prakriti. Without the Prakritic touch, Jeevatma was one with Paramatma (Gita XV:7). When it has come in collision with Prakriti its consciousness (Chetana) and radiance got constrained (Gita XIII:7). This triggered the cycle of repeated births for the Jeevatmas (Gita XIII:22). Till the Jeevatma comes out of the Prakritic constraints, it can't regain the true wisdom. The three primitive qualities namely Satvik, Rajasik and Tamasik that Jeevatma carries are triggering an endless chain of actions. When Jeevatma visualizes a state above the three primitive qualities of Prakriti, then he starts beholding and experiencing Paramatma (Gita XIV:19,20).

The purpose of the manifestation of mother nature (Prakriti) is to offer tools for the nourishment of the individual souls for their salvation (Sankhya karika Verse 57). Individual souls carry the seeds and impressions of Paramatma (Gita VII:10). Prakriti nourishes Jeevatma till it becomes equivalent to Paramatma.

One who utilizes the tools of the Prakriti in a right manner will be able to understand the purpose of his life and end goal for his journey. Satvik quality of the Prakriti accelerates the self-realization by connecting the individual with the Divine path, whereas the Tamasik quality constraints the intellect (Gita XIV:6,8). What to choose from the Prakriti is in the hands of individual.

It is not an easy task for the Jeevatma to get liberated (Gita VII:19, IV:5, VII:3). This is because, in the effort to the utilize the Prakritic elements, when Jeevatma stirs the 24 facets of Prakriti, the effort gets mixed up with three prime energies namely Satvik, Rajasik and Tamasik in different proportions. These three prime qualities form as veil of Maya (delusion) there by obscuring the intellect of the individual from Atman within (Gita VII:14). This veil of delusion disables the ability of individual Jeevatmas from effortlessly beholding the Paramatma. This cripples the true power of Individual and thus restricts his true ability and confines him to the generic attributes of the birth that he or she has taken. Thus, Prakriti is offering two paths for the individual. First path is to use its tools to realise Soul within and the second path is to use its tools to indulge in the activities which satisfy body & mind. Individual is free to choose the path (Gita V:14).

When the mind chooses the second path mentioned above, the intellect of individual gets disconnected from the spark of Atman, and gets immersed in the infinite ocean of Maya. It starts exploring various avenues for life's comfort. Ideally intellect should tune with Atman, however due to the veil of delusion, intellect is taken over by the mind. Mind which acts as the owner of the body starts creating a false 'I' or false identification for the body. This is ego which makes us to identify ourselves with body. Mind prioritizes the decision based on the temperament and qualities that the individual nurtured over his or her past births. Thus, Atman within gets buried under the delusion, and its guidance to the intellect becomes dim. On the other hand, Mind which is under constant agitation takes over the charge of the body.

Knowingly or unknowingly, everyone is in the quest for Satvik conditions of peace and tranquillity and progressing in that direction. Upon lessons learned in various births on disadvantages of Rajasik and Tamasik qualities, individuals slowly turn towards Satvik nature and thus slowly starts experiencing the peace in the lap of Prakriti through Satvik deeds of truthfulness, righteousness, forgiveness & compassion (Gita VII:19). Slowly the individual sails away from platforms of chaos to avenues of peace and tranquillity (Gita XIV:20). To such persons all the fluctuations of the mind are stilled. Their mind's response to what they see and listen is stems from the intellect given by Jeevatma within. At this state, the 24 attributes of the mother nature become irrelevant as consciousness is now tuned with the Jeevatma (Gita II.52). Slowly and steadily the individual moves to a level where Satvik quality also vanishes and the consciousness of individual reaches a state of pure bliss where none of the Satvik, Rajasik and Tamasik strains persists (Patanjali Yoga Sutras IV:34). For such a matured soul, Prakriti becomes irrelevant. Prakriti thus relieves him which is called the state of Salvation or Kaivalya. In that state Jeevatma establishes direct communion with Paramatma without being mediated by Prakriti.

In the state of Liberation, Jeevatma establishes direct com-munion with Paramatma. Once such a state is reached, Jeevatma don't need Prakritic tools any more (Patanjali Yoga Sutra IV:34 & Gita XIII:34).

Jeevatma which has not reached such a level of self-consciousness, will be dragged back again and again by Prakriti. It will be nourished by Pra-kriti and will be given one more chance by it. This cycle continues till the evolution of the Jeevatma is complete. The Individual soul within is carrying the seed of Paramatma himself. Like fire in the Yagna (sacred fire lit to invoke Divinity) rages with fuel offered to it, yet retains its sanctity and purity, in the similar manner sensory organ, human mind keeps fuelling the Jeevatma (Gita IV:26,27). Thus, with the Prakritic elements as the feed, Jeevatma lit the body making the body as sacred Yagna pot (Yajurveda: Sri Rudram: 10th Anuvaka of Chamaka Patha).

Jeevatma and Prakriti together are performing Yagna outcome which is pervading our body as a life force (Prana). Whether the individual is aware of it or not, the ongoing Yagna is to elevate the Atman to behold the Paramatma.

Sankhya school promotes the concept of Saguna Paramatma rather than the Nirguna Paramatma promoted by Vedanta. As per Sankhya, in the ultimate liberated state, Jeevatma dwells in eternal bliss and acquires all qualities of Paramatma while retaining its own identity (Gita XIV:27). So the Sankhya says that the seeds laid by Paramatma have resulted in the growth of many Purushas who are equal to him. ***This led to the riddle of Bahupurusha (many Paramatmas).*** Uttara Mimamsa especially Advaita philosophy is against this concept. However, Bhagavad Gita upheld both schools equally. There are many slokas in Bhagavad Gita which can be better understood with the Sankhya line of thought. For instance see Gita XIV 4, XV:17. There are other slokas in Bhagavad Gita which can be interpreted only with the Advaita line of thought. For instance, see Gita X:39,42, XIII:31.

Riddles Thrown by Sankhya School: Sankhya opens up the possibility of an infinite set of evolved Jeevatmas which acquired the dynamic equilibrium with that of Paramatma. After acquiring all the qualities of Paramatma, evolved Jeevatmas can trigger creation independent of the Paramatma from which originally, they branched out (Gita XV:17). They are like the aerial prop-up roots of the peepal tree that grows into a trunk and can later survive on their own even if the main root is not in contact with them. Similarly, the evolved Jeevatmas attain independence from their root in the same manner that of the propped-up root of the peepal tree (Gita XV:1, read along with the sloka Gita XIV:27). Thus, Sankhya not only indicates many Paramatmas, it also triggers the possibility of a multiverse. Those who read Devi Bhagavata of Sage Vyasa can better understand the concept of multiverse indications in ancient Indian texts. The difference between the Paramatma and the Jeevatma which has become equal to Paramatma is that the Paramatma is the one who never came in contact with the Prakriti (Patanjali Yoga Sutras Chapter I: 24), whereas the liberated souls were previously in contact with the Prakriti. Paramatma has never come in contact with time (Patanjali Yoga Sutras Chapter I: 26). He is the Prime Seed of the Universe and He is "OM[1]" (Patanjali Yoga Sutras Chapter I:27).

[1] *Author's Note: Probably modern-day mathematics like Set Theory and Number Theory can assist well in understanding the concept of the possibility of the existence of infinite number of infinities. As per the presently accepted notion, there can be small infinities and big infinities. There can be infinite number of infinities without overlapping each other. Bahu Purusha's concept of Sankhya, where each of the evolved souls is infinite in its own right yet not identical with the other, can be understood from modern-day mathematics.*

Those who are interested to know further about the Bahu Purusha concept of Sankhya are advised to read authentic texts on Sankhya. What is certain is 'for those Jeevatmas whose journey is complete, they reach the state of ecstasy and become equal to Paramatma'. This was repeatedly emphasized in Bhagavad Gita.

The Divine Trinity: Having given an overview of Sankhya Philosophy and its take on the Divine Trinity, subsequent sections will dwell more on attributes of each of these Divine Trinity namely Prakriti, Jeevatma and Paramatma.

Mother Nature or Prakriti or Sakti: She is the visible and invisible world (Gita X:42). Her consciousness has spread to every nook and corner of the universe. Everything visible and invisible are immersed in her (Gita XIII:14). Entire space of this universe hangs in her (Gita XI:20). She can extend a helping hand to the virtuous and can kick the wicked at any time (Gita XI:25). All those who are non-virtuous are running in an accelerated manner into her mouth only to get crushed under her teeth (Gita XI:27). *She is the one who commands and controls the Law of Karma.* Those who take refuge in her will find her in a pleasant posture with her beautiful and motherly face radiating solace and bliss (Gita XI: 10,11). Her grace and compassion can save individuals from their previous wrongdoings (Karma). For the righteous, she manifests herself in blissful forms (Gia XI:17,18) and for those who are wicked she may manifest in ruthless form (XI:25). Thus, she plays the role of administrator. She can see, touch, and listen to anything and everything in this universe as everything is immersed in her (Gita XIII:14). Though she is the source of all qualities of living and non-living beings, she is above all these qualities (Gita XIII:15). The dualities of near & far, small & big, inside & outside, moving & non-moving vanishes in her.

When the life span of a living being is over, she withdraws certain attributes from them and thus dissolves them in her. Thus she becomes the cause of death. For those souls which need to continue their journey of further evolution, she pulls them back into physical form by bestowing required attributes thereby becoming the source and cause of their birth (Gita XIII: 13-17,34,39). Like a thread running through the garland, she is the interconnecting thread between various births of individuals (Gita XIII:17, XIV:3,4). She knows what we are in our previous births and bestows us the present life based on the aggregate of our Karma (GitaVII:26). She manifests as wisdom in the learned, righteousness in the seekers, and the quality of highest virtue among the nobles (Gita X:37,38). She is the one who incites the right thoughts of love and compassion. She can become the most powerful weapon an individual can hold. She becomes the source of most valuable assets when sought truthfully (Gita X: 28). She is the one who nourishes the quality that an individual yearns for, like righteousness among the nobles, deceit among gamblers, the zeal for victory among the ambitious (Gita X:36). Her 24 attributes give all the required nourishment for the individual souls to prosper in their journey towards higher realms.

However, to make the evolutionary journey of Jeevatma meaningful and free from memories of pains and pleasures, she weaves a nest of delusion or Maya. Thus, she gives repeated chances for the Jeevatma to evolve and behold the Paramatma. The nest or veil of Prakriti is made up of three primitive qualities namely Satvik (Quality of Knowledge), Rajasik (Quality of Action) and Tamasik (Quality of inaction and ignorance). This veil (Maya) obscures the individual's view of the true self. Like an unborn baby in the womb, surrounded by the umbilical liquid of the mother, all the living and non-living beings are submerged in mother nature's 24 qualities and the veil of Maya cast by her. She has infinite facets which are beyond the imaginative power of an individual (Gita X:40). Human mind can't comprehend what is beyond mother nature as the mind and intellect of an individual are part of mother nature's attributes (GitaX:34). It is difficult for any individual to look beyond the veil unless he is trained under a learned teacher. Other way around, individuals can follow the path of enlightened souls to overcome the veil of delusion. This invokes divinity within and guides him on how to seek refuge at the feet of Prakriti upon which she will guide us on how to swim across the ocean of ignorance, and delusion that she has created (Gita VII:14).

In short, she is the one who provides all resources, judges one's actions, and supports the activities of each individual irrespective of their intent (thus giving freedom to individuals to pursue their good or bad choices). She acts as a judge thereby bestowing the rewards or punishments as per the Law of Karma. She doesn't have any special affection or hatred towards any individual (Gita IX:29). All the incarnations (Lord Rama, Lord Krishna, Lord Hanuman) that have manifested in a shape & form with specific attributes are manifestations of Mother nature herself. She takes the physical form on this earth whenever it is essential to set the course of nature back to track (Gita IV:7).

Mother nature or Prakriti has two facets, they are Lower Prakriti and Higher Prakriti. The lower Prakriti is manifested through the 23 qualities (except the Mahat which is the unmanifest form). Higher Prakriti (Mahat) dictates the beginning and the end of the creation (Gita VII:4-6). It dictates the manifestation of Lower Prakriti and the individual souls. During the beginning of the cycle of creation, Higher Prakriti is the one which brings the individual souls and keeps them in the womb of lower Prakriti and thus becomes the cause of the birth of all individual beings (Humans, Gods/ Devas etc,) (Gita XIV:3). The lower Prakriti has a beginning and has end whereas the higher Prakriti don't have a beginning and the end. In the Hindu line of thought, the facet of Prakriti that brings Pralaya (end of creation) is represented by Kali. She is the one who controls the time and she is the time. Each cycle of creation is represented as the skull around the neck of Kali (Gita VII:6). The skull of garlands that hangs around the neck of Kali symbolizes the representation of many previous manifestations that have dissolved in Higher Prakriti.

I am the all-consuming death (Gita VII:6). I am the prosperity of the prosperous (Gita XIII:34). I appear in a blissful form to the righteous and in a fierce form to the wicked (Gita XI:10,25)

Having discussed the attributes of Prakriti in detail, now let us see what are the attributes of Jeevatma.

Individual Soul/ Jeevatma (Divinity within): This is the second in the hierarchy of the Divine trinity. Sankhya school proposes that evolution can't happen without a purpose. It says that *the purpose of coming together of primitive energies of nature in an organised manner should be for a purpose, there should have been someone to ride the three primitive energies of Prakriti. Since there must be someone to feel the outcome of the acts, Jeevatma must exist as the owner of the body (Sankhya Karika: Verse 17).*

Bhagavad Gita says that there is a Soul within the body as a conscious force feeling the pleasures and pains of the outcome of various activities (Gita: XIII:21). Prakriti is the mother of Jeevatma and Paramatma is its father (Gita: XIV:3,4). Attributes of Jeevatma overlap and entangle with the 24th attribute of mother nature (intuition or Mahat) and present as the spark of life in the body. Though it is different from the 24 attributes of mother nature, it utilizes these attributes to manifest. It is also beginning and endless like the mother nature herself (Gita II:21, XIII:20). It can't be cut into pieces, it can't be burnt with fire, it can't be touched by air, it can't be wet with water, it can't be cut into pieces. It is eternal, immovable and present from the beginning of the creation (Gita II: 23,24). Using the 24 attributes and three basic qualities offered by the Prakriti as tools, it starts experiencing the pleasures and pains (Gita XIII:21). It should not be confused with the Spark of the Paramatma (Maheswara or Parampurusha) which is present in the body as an onlooker and supervisor. Paramatma is the master who is witnessing the indulgence of the Individual soul as an onlooker (Gita XIII:23).

When the Jeevatma entangles with the Prakriti, three basic energies of Prakriti namely Satvik (quality of peace and Divinity), Rajasik (quality of energy, ambition, and passion), Tamasik (quality of Inaction, ignorance) throw a veil of delusion on it. This triggers the dualities of life on Jeevatma. Due to its association with mother nature's attributes, it is immersed in them and imbibes the dualities of lower Prakriti (Gita XIII: 22). After acquiring the dualities (good & bad, wisdom & ignorance etc) it has fallen in the realm of cycles of birth and death (Gita XIII:22). Due

83

to the dualities imbibed from Prakriti, Jeevatma starts enjoying pleasures and feels pain. It identifies the near & far, in & out, small & big, and moving & non-moving due to its association with various attributes of mother nature (Lower Prakriti).

As the seed source of the individual Jeevatma is the Almighty (super soul) himself, it has all the attributes of the Almighty as well. It can be present devoid of three primitive qualities of Prakriti. However, like a new born doesn't acquire sufficient knowledge of his true nature, thus confined to the mother's lap, the individual soul which acts as an owner of the body carries body consciousness (consciousness of Prakriti) than the consciousness that has to be nurtured beyond the body. Thus, Jeevatma starts dwelling in Lower Prakriti which is in its immediate vicinity as it can be felt effortlessly. It owns false identification of pleasures & pains and other dualities of life as its true nature (Gita XIII:21). However, its true nature has many other attributes which are beyond any of the 24 attributes that it was associated with.

When the body it has occupied deteriorates, the soul within leaves the body and finds a new body for its manifestation (Gita II-22). It is beginningless, eternal, and never dies even when the body that it occupies vanishes (Gita II:20). In every cycle of birth, it acquires and accumulates an incremental degree of wisdom or ignorance. There are many realms, where individual souls having evolved to different degrees live and thrive. The realm of Gods is Devaloka (the sphere of light and ecstasy), the realm of demons is Adholoka (the sphere of darkness and distress), the realm in which we are present is Manusha loka (a transition sphere from darkness to light, ignorance to knowledge, distress to ecstasy). Jeevatma keeps moving between the upward and downward realms based on various attributes it has acquired from Mother nature. In the Manushaloka (the world where humans are living), human beings are dependent on other living and non-living things of the world for their survival, and the individuals in Devaloka (a world where heavenly beings stay) are dependent on the Manushaloka for their survival. They receive the offerings made in the Manushaloka to sustain their Divine energy of light and ecstasy. In turn, they shower their blessings on the Manushaloka (Gita III:11). However, those who are not offering or saluting to these celestial beings (Devas) for what was given to them, and enjoying all the wealth for selfish causes, are like a thieves who stole the wealth of someone and thus incurring sin. By being thankful to the Gods, by offering salutations to them, by offering part of one's rightful earning to the Divine cause, Jeevatma can promote the Divinity within as it is following the mandate of Almighty defined for those in Manushaloka (Gita III:13).

Godhood of Super Soul (Paramatma): He has two facets. First among them is neither having form nor formless. He is different from the both. He is the ultimate truth and primordial seed hailed by Vedas (Gita XV:18). Brahma is the word used for Paramatma by Vedanta School. He is the primitive cause of the universe. He is referred to as Purushottama or Maheswara (Gita XV:17). He is the primordial sound "OM". He can't be perceived as long as Jeevatma is identifying itself as

85

a mere body. Paramatma is the essence of Vedas (Ref: Chadyogapanishad, First Chapter). He is the highest form of song and music one can bask in (Ref: Udgita, Chadyogapanishad). During the creation of this universe, Maheswara acted as a father and rained individual souls into the womb of mother nature (Gita XIV:4). Thus, he is the father of the universe. He is the ultimate Divine power and the noblest of all the manifestations of the Almighty. Everything else in this universe including Prakriti is hanging in him (Gita XV:17). *Vedas and Scriptures called him as noble among Purushas (Purshottama) as He was never touched by any of the 24 qualities of the Prakriti.*

Mother nature always worships him in many ways. She sings the song of OM in the form of blowing wind, with the sounds of lightning and thunderstorm, in the form of the sound of rain, and waves of oceans. Even when all the above stops the underlying silence of Prakriti hums the OM (Ref: Chadyogapanishad Second Chapter). One who understands this aspect and beholds this truth is the one who can immerse in him and can come out of the illusionary veil of Prakriti (Gita XV:19,20).

The second facet of the Paramatma is the visible form he assumes from the 'OM' with all noble qualities. He is the repository of all noble qualities. Out of many of his qualities, his compassionate quality has made him enter into the body of humans along with the individual soul. Staying in the body yet untouched by it, he acts as a lighthouse for the individual soul which is struggling in the ocean of the 24 qualities. While the Eswara (Individual soul) is the owner of the body, the super soul acts as

Maheswara guiding the individual soul out of the darkness. Like Sun alone is lighting and nourishing this entire earth, the same way Maheswara is lighting up all beings (Gita XIII:34,31).

Thus, there are two souls. One is the Individual soul (Jeevatma) and the other one is the Super soul (Paramatma). The individual soul may lose itself during the final stages of the evolution (Kaivalya/Liberation) in the deep contemplation of the Paramatma (and thus can be considered to have lost its identity) while the Maheswara is never lost himself hence considered as Akshara (eternal) (Gita XV:16).

Non-perishable purusha in the form of Maheswara travels along the individual souls throughout their journey as an inseparable companion. The Jeevatma gets entangled in the veil of maya. It cheers out during pleasures and moans during pain. It despairs at the will of destiny (Law of Karma) and surrenders to it leading to repeated cycles of birth and death. It's companion soul that is Paramatma serenely watches the entire play that is unfolding. When the Jeevatma looks at the serenity being enjoyed by the companion soul, it starts to wriggle out of the net of delusion and thus starts trekking the path of salvation (Mundaka Upanishads 3.1.1). It is to be noted here that, Some Hindu Schools of thought like Uttara Mimamsa called Maheswara as higher Prakriti.

Liberation is the state where the individual soul identifies itself with the super soul. To attain such a state, one has to burn the veil made of three qualities before leaving this body (Gita XIV:20).

Various Sects of Hindu Thought: The state of liberation and the role of Prakriti in the evolution of the individual soul, are the areas of debate between various schools of Hindu thought. Subtle differences of opinion on the Jeevatma, Prakriti and Paramatma lead to various sects in Hinduism. Following sections dwell further on this.

Advaita (Non-Dualistic) Thought and its Assessment of Divine Trinity: Advaita proposes that, everything that exit is Paramatma. Paramatma is the only truth. All other things including the visible and invisible universe are a delusion. There is no multiplicity of Godhood. The distinction between Paramatma, Prakriti (mother nature) and Jeevatma (Individual Atma) in reality does not exist. This distinction is born out of ignorance (Avidya). Brahma (Paramatma or Super soul) is not a being (Refer to Kenopanishad). Brahma is infinite, indivisible and devoid of any attributes and qualities. The visible world (Mother nature), sensual feelings, and dualities of life like happiness and sorrow, heat and cold etc. are real as long as ignorance exists. Ignorance triggers the feeling of multiplicity which in reality does not exit. When ignorance fades away the multiplicity vanishes and the oneness will prevail.

Thus, the world is real as long as ignorance prevails over the intellect. This is called in some Indian texts 'Vyavaharika Satta'. World becomes unreal when intellect blossoms and tunes with the Brahma. This is called in Advaita texts as 'Paramarthika Satta'. As per Advaita philosophy liberation is to tune with the ultimate reality which involves overcoming the maya or illusion born out of ignorance. Infinite and non-dual truth

88

is the only thing that exists and the *Jeevatma losses its false identity when one moves beyond ignorance.* As this experience is not mediated by senses it is a super sensual experience which is called in Upanishads as Aparoksha Anubhava (Refer Brihadaranyaka Upanishad 3.5.1).

As per this school, Prakriti and its 24 qualities are nothing but a play (Leela in Sanskrit) of Brahma. The multiplicity of individual souls and the Prakriti that appeared to be true are part of the play projected by Paramatma. As part of the play the Jeevatmas manifest, then evolves and finally behold the 'True Knowledge (Swarupa Gnana). In the process, many Jeevatmas immerses in the play so deeply that, they forget their true nature and start identifying with the role they are playing (Bhranti/delusion). They start feeling the pains and pleasures out of illusions. Brahma or Paramatma is the Pure consciousness (Chit) which can independently exist. Upon beholding the Brahma, delusionary play vanishes.

A simple parable that explains Advaita is "Rajju Sarpa Bhati (confused identity of Rope as Serpent). Under the twilight when someone notices a rope, he may falsely feel it as a snake and get scared of it. When someone brings a light there, he realizes it is a rope and gets relaxed. There is no snake at any moment, it was a mere delusion and all reactions done under such a delusive state are out of ignorance. On the same lines, Advaita proposes that the world (Prakriti) that we see is a delusion. When one wakes up from a dream, he realizes the futility of what he experienced in the dream. Similarly, when one sees things in the wakeful state of true knowledge, Jeevatma (Individual soul) realizes its oneness with Paramatma (Super soul). Paramatma is attributeless, formless, shapeless, omnipresent, omnipotent, and eternal. Gaudapada and Adisanakaracharya are the main proponents of this school of Philosophy (For further reading please Refer to "Four Basic Principles of Advaita Philosophy" by Swami Bhajananda, Ramakrishna Mutt, Prabuddhabharata Jan/Feb2010).

Proponents of Advaita School: Adisankara Charya, Chandra Sekharendra Saraswati, Swami Vivekananda

As per this school, Paramatma can be worshipped in either of the six Divine forms namely Lord Siva, Goddess Parvati, Lord Ganesha, Lord Karthikeya and Lord Vishnu, the Sun God and their other manifestations (Avatars). These are the forms of Almighty approved by Vedas for Upasana (to worship and meditate upon). Rest all Divine forms are subordinate to these forms. It upholds the Vedas, Upanishads, and Brahma sutras as the standard texts for understanding the Almighty. Puranas and Agamas are not accepted by this school as authentic. Yet this school identifies the need for Puranas, Agamas & Itihasas to convey the essence of philosophy to the masses in simple terms. Followers of this school are called 'Smartas'.

There are four seats of learning for this school of thought spread across India from where this philosophy is propagated. They are Sringeri in the south, Puri in the east, Dwaraka in the west, and Badri ashram in the north. Kanchi is also the seat of this tradition.

Vaishnava School of Thought: This school of thought proposes that Paramatma is Lord Vishnu. As per this school of thought, rest all Divine manifestations are subordinate manifestations of Lord Vishnu. This school also gives primacy to Vedas, Upanishads and Brahma sutras as authentic texts to understand the Almighty. Followers of this school of thought are called Vaishnavas. There are different sects in the Vaishnava school. They are Dvita (Dualistic) school, Visistadwaita (Qualified Monism), Suddhadvaita (Pure Nondualism), Achintya Bheda Abheada School (Inconceivable Oneness) and Vaikhanasa school. How the trinity of Godhood (Paramatma, Jeevatma and Prakriti) are seen by the Vaishnava schools is elaborated below.

Dvaita (Dualistic) School of Thought: It was propounded by Madhvacharya. It promotes the concept of the existence of two realities of which one is an independent reality (Paramatma) and the other is a dependent reality which includes both Prakriti and Jeevatma. It states that Paramatma is Lord Vishnu. There is no peer or superior to him (Ref; Chadyogapanishad). He is the first and independent reality.

Jeevatmas are dependent on Paramatma. Lord Vishnu knows the beginning of the Jeevatmas (Gita IV:4). This school says that the rest of the Gods are evolved Jeevatmas including Goddess Lakshmi. Other Gods can be worshipped if it is done with a feeling that, through these Gods, the prayers are sent to Lord Vishnu. Any prayer done independently to any other God other than Vishnu is an apostasy.

Paramatma is having a body and form made of Satchidananda (a Mix of Existence, Consciousness and bliss). He is the repository of all noble qualities, he is eternal. He governs and controls the worlds (various realms like heaven, earth etc). Jeevatmas (individual souls) are part of Paramatma, and thus dependent entities (Ref: https://www.britannica.com/topic/Dvaita, Accessed on 15th May 2021). Prakriti is part of Paramatma. It has manifested out of Paramatma. Hence Prakriti itself is also a dependent manifestation of the independent manifestation that is Paramatma. Chadyogapanishad makes one of the four grand pronouncements "Tatvamasi". Advaita school refers to this grand pronouncement (Mahavakya) as an inference for saying the Jeevatma and Paramatma are the same, the Dvaita school says that it is the grand pronouncement made to declare that Prakriti and Paramatma are the same! *(Ref: Prakpaschima Tatvasastra Charitra, Patr I, Telugu Version Compiled by Saripella Viswanadha Sastri Andhra Saraswata Parishad Publications, 1961).* This sect promotes Devotion (Bhakti) towards Lord Vishnu as the way to salvation. As per this school, Soul maintains its identity as a spark in Paramatma. Followers of this sect are called Madhvas.

Vallabhacharya (Suddhadvaita or Pure Nondualism) and Chaitanya Prabhu (Achintya Bhedabheda) are other proponents of Vaishnavism. These two sects promote Krishna Bhakti as the way of Salvation. (Ref: https://en.wikipedia.org/wiki/Shuddhadvaita accessed on 16th May 2021). They believe that Jeevatma and Prakriti are part of Paramatma, however, all the attributes of Paramatma are not reflected in them. As per these sects, salvation (Moksha) is to reach Krishna loka (abode of Krishna) and involve in his service. Even after salvation, the identity of Jeevatma is retained. Followers of Vallabhacharya are Gosains. Chaitanya Mahaprabhu's tradition has become popular throughout the world with the establishment of ISKCON (International Society for Krishna Consciousness). Puri Jagannath Temple and Vrindavan are the most revered places for the followers of ISKCON.

Both the Suddhadwaita and ISCKON traditions initiate the followers with 'Krishna Mantra (chant)' which they recite devotedly every day. The chanting and dancing of ISKCON devotees in the Divine ecstasy are worth watching and participating in.

As per these schools, Moksha or Salvation is to reach the Krishna loka and serve the Lord. Gopikas dancing in ecstasy is a representation of the Jeevatmas experiencing the bliss of the company of Paramatma. It is a typical depiction of the souls which have attained Moksha. This state is attained after getting liberated from the veil of delusion thrown by Prakriti.

It is easy to overcome all distractions for those who worship me with utmost devotion. They will reach my abode and relish in my company (Gita XIV:26,27, V:21)

Visistadwaiata Line of Vaishnavism: It promotes that the Jeevatma has got independent existence, yet at the same time inseparable from Paramatma. It can be compared to a light coming from a lamp. The light is an inseparable attribute of a lamp at the same time it has got its separate existence. Thus, the source of Jeevatmas is Paramatma. Jeevatma is a spark of Paramatma, yet it has got required attributes to acquire infinite knowledge. As per this school, Paramatma is a repository of noble qualities. He is not Nirguna (devoid of qualities). He has form and he is the repository of infinite noble qualities including Purity, Ultimate Reality & Wisdom

Proponents of Visistadwaita: Rananujacharya (on left) & Seer
Chinna Jeeyar Swamy

As per this school, the 24 qualities of Prakriti are real and permanent, and Paramatma is above the Prakriti. It promoted the concept of plurality of Jeevatmas. In the state of salvation, Jeevatma reaches the abode of the Paramatma and feels itself as an integral part of Paramatma. To reach to this level Jeevatma has to climb a nine stepped ladder mainly consisting of discretion, reluctance to indulge in false sensory pleasures, feeling of detachment (Karma Yoga), being scared of sin and its consequences, seeking the grace of Paramatma, ability to burn the clutches of Karma with the fire lit by the devotion etc--. Person who takes these steps will see a shining road to the abode of Paramatma. *(Ref: Visistadwaita: A Philosophy of Religion by K R Paramahansa. TTD Publications 2010).* Sri Ramanuja was the main proponent of Visistadwaita.

Vaikhanasa line of Vaishnavism: Vaikhanasa means digging deep. It promotes digging deep into Godhood present within through earnest contemplation assisted by worship. (Ref: Sri Vaikhanasa Bhagavata Sastram: An Introduction by SriRamakrishnaDikishituluebookhttp://www.sr_hayagrivan.org/ebooks/031_sva_v1p1.pdf). This is different from other schools of Vaishnavism as, it doesn't ponder too much on Upanishads, Bhagavad Gita and Brahma Sutras (Prasthana Traya) but rather relies on unwavering devotion towards Lord Vishnu. The followers of this line believe that the way to salvation need not pass through philosophical refinement.

This school believes that, instead of pondering over philosophy, the best practice for salvation is to worship Lord Vishnu with unwavering devotion. As per the followers of this path, Lord Vishnu himself revealed how to perform the rituals to his Divine forms to Lord Brahma in a conversation at Naimisaranya through a dialogue consisting of 32 questions. The knowledge gained by Lord Brahma was passed on to his disciples in the form of Vaikhanasa agama (Also called Vaikhanasa

Bhagavata Sastra) which even today is devotedly implemented by followers of this sect. Tirupati is their main seat of learning.

Leave behind the path of deep Philosophical explorations, nurture unwavering devotion towards Almighty. He will take care of your every need. (Essence of Vaikhanasa School)

This school believes that, Jeevatma can't comprehend the vastness (non-iconic form) of Paramatma. What Jeevatma can comprehend is the Sakala form or iconic form (vastness of the Paramatma represented by a graceful). Prakriti is the source of power for the Sakala form of Lord Vishnu. Salvation means Jeevatma reaching the abode of Lord Vishnu through devoted rituals to the Sakala form of Paramatma.(Ref: https://en.wikipedia.org/wiki/Vaikhanasas accessed on 22nd May 2021

& https://hinduism.stackexchange.com/questions/3977/what-is-the-story-of-vikhanasa-founder-of-the-vaikhanasa-school, accessed on 22nd May 2021).

Saivitic Schools of Thought: As per these schools of thought Paramatma is Lord Siva and the rest of all Divine manifestations are subordinate manifestations to Lord Siva. This school also gives primacy to Vedas, Upanishads and Brahmasutras as authentic texts to understand the Almighty. However certain subsects of this school of thought give equal or even primacy to Saiva agamas as well. Agamas are "discourses of Siva to Sakti". These schools believe that Siva is pure consciousness and that the Sakti is the manifested form of Siva. There are different sects in the Saivitic school. Kashmiri Saivism, Pasupata Saivism, Srouta Saivism, Veera Saiva, Lingayatism, Saiva Siddhanta or Sivadwaita Saivism, Nadh Saivism, Aghora Saivism etc. How the trinity of Godhood (Paramatma, Jeevatma and Prakriti) are seen by each of the Saivitic schools is elaborated below. Though Guru Sishya (Teacher and Disciple) tradition is prevalent in all sects of Hinduism, Saivitic schools emphasise on it is more than other schools. Yoga and mysticism are part of the Saivitic schools.

Kashmiri Saivism and Its Mysticism: Saiva Agamas or Tantras which were believed to be told by Lord Siva (Paramatma) himself to Mother Goddess Sakti (Prakriti) are the basis for this school. Vasu Gupta and Abhinav Gupta were the famous proponents of this school which flourished between the 9th century to 14th century AD. This school believes that everything that is visible is the mere transformation of consciousness into different entities. Each entity is made up of Siva (Paramatma) and Sakti (Prakriti). This school calls Siva as 'Bhairava' and Sakti as 'Bhairavi'. Sakti or Prakriti is the platform which provides Jeevatmas, the means for attaining the union with Siva". Jeevatmas are reflections of Lord Siva (Paramatma) and are having contracted consciousness about their true nature. Siva and Sakti can't exist without each other. Unlike the Advaita school, Kashmiri Saivism states that Sakti is real, permanent and has its own will. Siva is energy in the unmanifest form, whereas Sakti is the manifest form of energy with independent will (Swatantra). Sakti has its manifestations at three levels which are Para (Supreme), Parapara (intermediate) and Apara (inferior). To behold the intermediate and supreme states of the Sakti, one needs to invoke the eye of wisdom or the third eye.

Siva and Sakti are inseparable. Sakti is the manifest form of Siva

Everyone carries a third eye as every Jeevatma is a reflection of Siva who has a third eye. This eye can be opened either with the blessing of the Guru or with the blessings of the Supreme Lord (Bhagavad GitaXI:8). This eye will open the vision into Divine realms. There are more than a hundred methods of Dharana (concentration) through which one can open the third eye as stated in the "Vignana Bhairavam", which is one of the standard books that deal with Kashmiri Saivism.

•The state of inner blissful experience is inexpressible with words. It is the state of Bhairava which is free from space, time and form. This state is full of energy (Bhairavi) and inner bliss (Bhairava). It is the state where sound ends and hence it is soundless (Nadanta). Various methods recommended to attain this blissful state in the 'Vignana Bhairavam' are classified into three categories namely 'Sambhavopaya, Saktopaya and Anavopaya'. Depending on the evolution of the seekers Guru should prescribe a suitable method. These methods ignite the Kundalini (the life force) and guide its ascension through six Divine states of consciousness ultimately leading to the Sahasrara where the life force beholds the true nature of Siva or Bhairava. As per Kashmir Saivism, this state is the state of Pratyabhijna or the state of recognizing the true nature. For the benefit of the readers, a few methods of concentration recommended by Kashmiri Saivism are given below from Vignana Bhairavam.

•A typical Saktopaya recommends "Fix the eyes on a particular object, withdraw the thoughts from all other objects and focus on the object identified for the focus, slowly withdraw the gaze from even this single object, its knowledge and thought". Then the void of material thoughts that form will be filled by the consciousness of Siva.

•Another Saktopaya method of awakening Siva consciousness recommended is to "Perceive the vastness of the universe around you, feel the vast universe in all 360 degrees around you with innumerable stars and galaxies, feel how you are hanging in this vast universe". This will expand the consciousness of the individual to tune with the consciousness of Siva.

•A typical Sambhavopaya recommends "Nurture the intense devotion which should lead to indifference towards all other things". In such a state it is possible to tune with the energy of Sankari (Goddess Parvati) which will ensure the consciousness of Lord Siva.

•Wherever the mind finds satisfaction let it be fixed there. The nature of the supreme soul will manifest there and then. Do not think of any act as superior or inferior Fix the mind where it finds peace. In such acts which rejoice the mind, the sense organs become an instrument for worship. Thus, they unite us with the ultimate bliss of Brahma (Tantra Loka IV: 120-121)

Kashmiri Saivism says that to reach the state of Siva Consciousness, meditation is not the only way. Siva consciousness can be attained through any means like music or dance or any other aesthetic means where our mind overcomes all other distractions and allows us to focus on one particular thought. Kashmiri Saivism doesn't accept the concept of maya (illusion) and ignorance (avidya) proposed by the Advaita school. It proposes that ignorance and illusion are some of the many facets of Prakriti which are real. Maya is a personified Prakriti. It is real for all enslaved Jeevatmas (called Pasu). Those who tune themselves with Siva's (referred to as 'Pati') consciousness can come out of this enslavement.

"When the mind of Yogi is one with the unparalleled joy of music or any other aesthetic delights, then Yogi is identified with it due to expansion of mind which has merged in attributes of Paramatma" (Ref: Vignana Bhairava – The Practice of Centring Awareness by Swami Lakshman Joo. Method 73, Page 95 Indica Publishers)

Kashmiri Saivism does not accept conventional Sankhya and even Advaita schools on who is the 'Doer'?. As per Sankhya and Vedanta, intellect (Buddhi) is the doer. Since intellect is also part of Prakriti, it is the Prakriti that is the doer. Jeevatma only experiences the pleasures and pains of actions. However, Kashmiri Saivism identifies Jeevatma as the doer.

For more details on Kashmiri Saivism readers are recommended to refer to *"Vignana Bhairava: The Practice of Centering Awareness, Commentary by Swami Lakshman Joo, Compiled by Bettina Baumer"*. Those who want to understand the mystic aspects of the Bhagavad Gita from the viewpoint of Kashmiri Saivism are recommended to study Abhinava Gupta's Commentary on the Bhagavad Gita under the title "Gitartha Sangraha" translated from Sanskrit to English by Boris Marjanovic (Indica Publishers, Varanasi).

Srouta Saiva School: This school preaches Sivadwaita. It is close to Visistadwaita but with subtle differences which are elaborated on in this section. It derives its philosophical thoughts from Vedas, Upanishads and Brahma sutras hence it is also identified as Srouta Saiva. The precursor for all the Saivitic schools is Pasupata Saivism. Srouta Saiva school also owes its relation to Pasupata school. There are references to Pasupata Saivitic tradition in Mahabharata as well. Historically, Pasupata Saivism was prevalent in Northern India during the reign of Samudra Gupta (as inferred from the Lakulisacharya's Mathura Inscription dated 200 BCE). It has the Guru (Spiritual Teacher) and Sishya (Disciple) tradition starting from the Sadasiva himself, moving down through Parasara, Badarayana (the compiler of Brahma Sutras) & Kapila.

Pasupata Saivism in its original form was prevalent in the Telugu-speaking areas of India till the Tamil Saivitic movements and Kashmiri Saivitic movements penetrated these lands. This can be inferred from the fact that 'Sivatatva Saram' written by Mallikarjuna Panditaradya (who lived around the 11th century AD) identified the Saivitic movement that he is preaching as the Pasupata Saivism (Ref: Commentary on Basava Puranam by Sri Veturi Prabhakara Sastry, TTD Publications 2013). Mallikarjuna Panditaradhya is one of the twelve learned teachers (Dwadasa Aradhyas) of present-day Srouta Saiva school. After Mallikarjuna Panditaradhya, this sect got strongly influenced by the Saivitic movements of Tamil land. This can be inferred from the book titled 'Panditaradhya Charitra' written by PalkurikSomanatha (Who lived during the 12th and 13th AD). This book promoted the Nayanars and their teachings on Sivadwaita, as well as the Pasupata Saivism. Palkuriki Somanatha was patronized by Kakatiya King Pratapa Rudra II (1140-1196 AD). Palkuriki Somanatha is one of the twelve learned teachers of the Srouta Saiva sect. The philosophical thoughts of Pasupata have a strong connection with Sankhya School. However, unlike the Sankhya school's Bahupurusha (multiple Godhood), Pasupata recognizes one ultimate God as Siva. These philosophical changes made by the Pasupata school to the Sankhya Philosophy got further refined when it passed through the Kashmiri Saivism. Abhinav Gupta's Tantra Loka has references to Pasupata Saivism. Kashmiri Saivism's philosophy flowed down throughout India. It has influenced the Saivitic movements of South India as well. The book titled "Udbhata Aradhya Charitra" was written by Tenali Ramalinga Kavi who belongs to Srouta Saiva school and is a court poet of Sri Krishna Devaraya of the 16th Century AD. In this book, he has written that the great Saivitic teacher from the Gharjara Kingdom and who was the Guru of the then Kashmir King (Jayapida 779 to 813 AD) propagated the Saivitic school that he was following.

Thus, with the confluence of thoughts from the Sankhya school, Pasupata Saivism, Kashmiri Saivism, & Tamil devotional movement a separate school of Hindu thought emerged and flourished in Telugu-speaking areas of India. It is recognized as Srouta Saivism or Aradhya Saivism. Srouta Saivism identifies 12 learned teachers who propagated this line of thought, they are called Dwadasa Aradhyas (12 enlightened souls, https://shaivam.org/devotees/dwaadasa-aaradhyas accessed on 27th June 2021). They include Revana Siddha, Neelakantharadhya (Commentator of Brahma Sutras under the title of Neelakantha Bhashyam), Lakuleesa Acharya, Viswaradhya, Sri Pati Panditaradhya etc. In recent times Srouta Saiva thought was propagated by the Great Gurus like Mudigonda Nagalinga Sastry, and Sadguru Kandukuri Sivananda Murthy. The present seer of the sect is His Holiness Sri Attaluri Mrityunjaya Sarma. Those who wish to see the unbroken chain of Siddhas (realized souls) of this tradition are recommended to visit Sri Gurudham at Balususpadu Village, Jaggaiahpet of Andhra Pradesh India where a God-realized soul Sri Venkata Ramana, the disciple of Sadguru Sivananda Murthy is staying.

Among the Upanishads, Svetaswatara Upanishad, among the six orthodox schools of Philosophy Sankhya School. Among various practices of yoga Patanjali yogic tradition is the basis for the Srouta Saiva School of thought. This school proposes Lord Siva as the Paramatma. It doesn't accept the concept of Prakriti as delusion rather it recognizes Prakriti as real and eternal. The role of Prakriti is to provide a platform for the evolution of Jeevatma to a level where it doesn't need any Prakritic elements for its evolution. At the state of Moksha, Jeevatma reaches the abode of Lord Siva. In the liberated stage Jeevatma experiences and beholds Siva in the form of unlimited bliss which is beyond the bliss one can derive from the tools of Prakriti (Prakritic bliss is derived from the quality of Satva, whereas the bliss experienced in the state of salvation is beyond the reach of Satvik quality). This school believes that the state of salvation is not attribute less rather it is attaining companionship with the Paramatma and imbibing his state of bliss (Taittiriya Upanishad 2.1.1). Svetaswatara Upanishad which hails Rudra as the eternal is referred to widely in the texts of this school.

Mystic Elements of Srouta Saiva School: Most of the other schools stop by saying that the Paramatma or Maheswara is present within our body along with the Jeevatma and salvation involves beholding the Paramatma. This school moved further ahead and says that there is an empty inner space in the heart (Dahara Akasa) (Patanjali Yoga Sutras Chapter IV:34). It is referred to as Brahma Nadi in ancient texts. By unknotting this, one can see the Maheswara sitting inside the heart (Patanjali Yoga Sutras: Chapter I:25). This can be achieved through utmost devotion and surrender (Patanjali Yoga Sutras Chapter I:23 & Svetasvatara Upanishad I:10). To turn attention towards Maheswara, one has to take the path of meditative absorption supported by the recitation of Mantra (Panchakshari mantra) while focusing the attention on

106

the cosmic form of Lord Siva represented by the Sivalinga as the iconic form (refer to Sadhya and Linga concept of Nyaya School under the Anumana Pramana). In this school, Guru hands over a small Sivalinga to the disciple for his/her daily meditation. To ensure that the Divine power is invoked in the Sivalinga, it passes through similar Vedic rites that are performed for a Sivalinga before it is installed in a temple. All these rites are conducted to a small Sivalinga under an evolved teacher who has progressed in this path. After the required Vedic rites, Guru initiates the devotee by giving the mantra and Sivalinga. Disciples wear the Sivalinga around their necks. This is called 'Sambhava Deeksha or Pasupata Deeksha'. Deeksha means an oath to practice something. This school believes that the practice of Sambhava Deeksha is the essence of recommendations made to seekers in Kalagni Rudropanishad/Atharva Sikhopanishad.

As per Patanjali Yoga Sutras meditation is defined as fixing the mind on one place (desa bandha), followed by fixing the mind on one image (Pratyaika tanata) Siva Linga worn by the seeker provides the required indicative direction to fix the mind quickly on to a single thought and on a single image. As per the Patanjali Yoga Sutras mind projects various images continuously. *As the mind fixes on one image, then the impression of the same image is projected uninterruptedly* (Patanjali Yoga Sutras: I:32, Chapter III: 1&2). *This is the state of meditative absorption*. Siva Linga assists this yogic practice. Hence such practice is followed in this school.

107

The same Sutras of Patanjali were referred by Vaishnavitic scholars in their commentaries to Patanjali Yoga Sutras while recommending meditation. They recommended fixing the concentration on the beautiful face of Hari. Patanjali has not mentioned specifically which object or image is to be used to assist the mind to fix itself. He has left it to the inclination of individuals (Patanjali Yoga Sutras: Chapter I:39). Saivitic scholars recommended focusing on Siva Linga while Vaishnavite schools promoted the image of Hari.

Initiation into the Sambhava Deeksha is an additional initiation other than sacred thread initiation (Upanayana). Sambhava Deeksha is also given to women devotees. The person who takes this initiation vows to practice daily Vedic rites through recitations of hymns related to the invocation of Lord Siva. This invokes the Sivatva in the Siva Linga that he carries. Over time, with their steadfast devotion to the Lord Siva, devotees progress to a stage where their intellect is absorbed by Siva, their soul starts feeling the presence of Siva, and their every activity is steadfastly surrendered at the feet of Siva. Their ego vanishes and dissolves in the ego of Maheswara. This is the first step to attain salvation (Gita V:17). Siva Linga that they carry and worship acts as a Divine spark that enables the individuals to lift their consciousness to Divine realms. Through steadfast devotion, they get cleansed of past sins and acquire the wisdom to unknot their soul from the Prakritic entanglements (Brahma Nadi). Once this Brahma Nadi is unknotted, Jeevatma is freed from the bondage of ignorance of Prakritic elements and reaches the abode of Lord Siva. The knot that is tying the Jeevatma as Pasu(ignorant) can be broken by the grace of Pati (Lord Siva or Pasupati). Hence this school is also called Pasupata.

The main seats of learning of this sect are Warangal, Srisailam, Saiva Maha Peetham at Hyderabad & Secunderabad, Vijayawada. This tradition doesn't promote Sanyasa deeksha which involves renouncing the family and other worldly attachments. It believes that Sanyasa is not an essential step for salvation. Hence the Gurus of this tradition are householders. This school differs from Veera Saivism in many aspects like Prakriti, Purusha, salvation, and authenticity of Vedic scriptures. However, both agree upon the Supremacy of Lord Siva, both wear Siva Linga, and promote the need for strong devotion towards Lord Siva for Salvation.

As per this tradition, there are three stages of salvation. They are Samipya moksha (Attaining the proximity of Lord Siva by reaching his abode that is Kailasa), Sarupya Moksha (attaining the form or formlessness close to Lord Siva) and Sayujya Moksha (starting to see the Universe through the eyes and feeling the creation through the heart of Lord Siva). Since the supreme being is identified as Siva, the spiritual aim of this school is to behold Siva and become equivalent to him. This school is also known as Ewaradwaita school to differentiate it from the Vaishnavitic schools of Visistadwaita.

Proponents of Srouta Saiva: Neelakantha Aradhya (top), Mudigonda Nagalinga Sastry (Centre) & Sadguru Sivananda Murthy (bottom).

Subtle Differences between Srouta Saiva with Visistadwaiata School and Advaita School on the Concept of Liberation or Moksha: The main difference between the Visistadwaita of Vaishnavism and that of Srouta Saivitic schools is that, as per the former school, even after the Salvation Jeevatma is not independent. At the state of salvation, Jeevatma recognizes its true self as part and parcel of the larger self which is primary Purusha. On the other hand, the Srouta Saiva school says that, after the liberation, the Jeevatma becomes independent and acquires all qualities of the primary Purusha. However, it stops short of accepting the Multiple Purushas (Bahu Purusha) and declares that Lord Siva is the ultimate Purusha. The difference between the Purusha who is liberated (Liberated Jeevatmas) and the Lord Siva (Prime Seed and Cause of Creation, thus primary Purusha) is that Lord Siva is Visesha Purusha who was never touched by time or other obstacles faced by Jeevatmas (Ref: Patanjali Yoga Sutras: Chapter I:24). Other obstacles like Karmic bonds that bind the Jeevatma never touched Lord Siva. Advaita school on the other hand says that after the liberation the Jeevatma doesn't retain its identity and dissolves in Paramatma.

The ground for debate and arguments between Advaita School and Srouta Saiva school over the centuries is summarized below. Readers are advised not to take any side but try to see the typical deep philosophical currents of various schools.

(i) Statement of Chadyogapanishad **"Bramhavit Bramhmaiva Bhavati"** is being interpreted by the Advaita school as the one who realizes

Brahma (Paramatma) becomes the Brahma itself. This is because, the Advaita school takes "**Eva bhavati**" as 'becoming the same' On the other hand, Srouta Saiva interprets it as the one who realizes that Brahma becomes similar to Brahma but not Brahma itself. Srouta Saiva school takes it as "**Iva Bhavati**" which in Sanskrit means 'Similar'. Readers who are interested to know more are advised to read the Paniniya grammar to take the correct meaning out of the above statement.

(ii) Statement from Brihadaranyaka Upanishad says "**Aham Brahmosmi**" which is being interpreted by the Advaita school as "I am the Brahma (Paramatma)" and there is no difference between the Jeevatma and Paramatma. Once the Jeevatma breaks the veil of delusion of Prakriti, it becomes the same with Paramatma. On the other hand, Srouta Saiva school says that, the full statement when read, it reads like "Tadatmana mevavit aham Brahmosmi iti" which means that the Brahma (Paramatma) relishes in his self and he doesn't need any of the 24 Prakritic tools to know that " I am the Brahma". Hence, it does not mean that the Jeevatma is realizing itself as Paramatma. A similar statement made in the Brihadaranyaka Upanishad in the "Upasana Prakarana" is only suggestive to the Upasaka (seeker) to contemplate Brahma with a feeling of oneness with him in terms of his qualities. It is commonly accepted practice for those who perform worship of Lord Siva through Vedic rites is to start their worship with the invocation of Lord Siva in their own body through special rites. Veda says that "Na rudro rudramarchate" (meaning one who wants to worship Lord Siva

112

can't do it without himself transforming as Siva). While reciting the Sri Rudram of Krishna Yajurveda, the devotees invoke the Sivatva (becoming one with Siva) in their bodies through various Mantras (hymns). While chanting the Gayatri Mantra the devotee invokes Goddess Gayatri in his own body through various Mantras. In a similar fashion one who is trying to contemplate the absolute Brahma or Paramatma should invoke Brahma with a feeling of "Aham Brahmosmi". Thus, Srouta Saiva says that "Aham Brahmosmi" does not mean the Jeevatma and Paramatma are the same, rather it is suggesting how to contemplate Brahma.

Those who wish to read more on the Saivitic interpretation of other Upanishadic statements like "Ayamatma Brahma (This soul is Brahma), " Tatvamasi (I am thee or I am the Brahma)" are advised to read the writings of the earliest teachers of this school like Nilakantha Aradhya, and modern-day scholars like Sri Mudigonda Nagalinga Sastry. On the other hand, those who wish to understand the line of thought of Advaita are advised to read the commentaries of Sri Sanakracharya and the teachings of the Rama Krishna Mission.

Some riddles thrown by each of these schools are projected below for the consumption of the readers so that they can understand how the focus on the state of Jeevatma at Moksha (liberation) has resulted in the evolution of various sects in Hinduism.

The general challenge to the Saivitic line of thought is that, if its version of liberation is accepted then it results in accepting "Bahu Purusha (Multiple Brahmas)". This is because each of the liberated souls when becomes equivalent to Brahma (Brahmavit Brahma 'iva' Bhavati) but not Brahma itself, then it leads to the existence of multiple Brahmas. This is close to the Sankhya school of thought which accepts the existence of multiple Brahmas. Patanjali Yoga sutras also lead to a similar conclusion as that of Sankhya philosophy indicating the existence of multiple Brahma. This is the reason why the Advaita Philosophy as a school doesn't accept the Sankhya philosophy.

On the other hand, if the Advaita school is accepted, it is to be accepted that, at the state of liberation, Jeevatma realises that it is none other than Paramatma himself and becomes one with him. If the Jeevatma present in all are the same, then it leads to a riddle. The riddle here is that, if the Jeevatma of one person attains Moksha (liberation), then the Jeevatmas of all others also should automatically graduate to Moksha as it is the same Jeevatma present in all beings. This is one of the grounds on which Sankhya school don't agree with Advaita Philosophy.

Probably the answer to these riddles should be known through own enlightenment instead of debate. Once enlightenment dawns, all these riddles will be answered.

Veerasaivism and Lingayat Schools of Saivism: This tradition follows pancha acharyas (Five enlightened teachers) who include Renukacharya, Darukacharya, Panditaradhya, Ekorama and Viswaradhya. There are subtle differences between Lingayatism and Veerasaivism. The latter promotes the philosophy close to Visistadwaita, but to differentiate it from other Vaishnavite schools of Visistadwaita, it is identified as "Sakti Visistadwaita". As per this school, Prakriti which acts as a platform for the evolution of souls is not an independent entity, rather it is Siva himself who transformed himself as Prakriti. This is also called "***Siva Brahma Parinama Vada***". As per this school, the world is not an illusion. It is the real manifestation of Siva himself. Veera Saivism is one of the oldest Saivitic schools. Those who want to study more on the Philosophy of Veerasaivism are advised to read "Sreekara Bhashyam"

On the other hand, Lingayatism was started by Lord Basaveswara. It promotes the "Soonya vada Siddhanta". As per this philosophy, the ultimate God is Siva, and he is devoid of any quality (Sunya Purusha). The terms Nada, Bindu and Kala are very significant in this philosophy. Nada represents Siva who is a static Divine (Sunya purusha). He needs Bindu which is Shakti (Prakriti) the dynamic divine to manifest. Due to the union of Siva and Sakti; Kala (time) and the Divine creation is born. As per this philosophy, the world is not an illusion. Human's final destiny or the purpose of existence is to know and to get united with the immanent and transcendent Godhead. This identification of the self with God or the Supreme can be achieved only by the death of the ego and elevation of the Soul. (https://www.virashaiva.com/philosophy-of-veerashaivism accessed on 26th June 2021). The state of Moksha is the union of Jeevatma with infinite and attribute less Siva (https://en.wikipedia.org/wiki/Lingayatism#cite_note-Panchacharyas_dating-9 accessed on 26th June 2021).

Though Srouta Saiva and Veera Saiva have some similarities they have many differences as well. The latter emphasizes Saiva Agama while not ignoring the Vedas & Upanishads, whereas the Srouta Saiva upholds Vedas and Upanishads as ultimate while not ignoring the Saiva Agamas. Srouta Saiva believes in the Saguna Siva (Sada Siva or the perpetual treasure of peace and transcendental bliss) whereas the Veera Saiva/Lingayat believes in the Siva who is Nirguna at the state of Moksha (Lingayatism New World Encyclopaedia, Accessed on 19th June 2022).

Lingayatism has broken the rigid Varna (caste) system and thus has become a reformation movement which promoted that anyone can attain liberation through the worship of Lord Siva. It believes in a six-step (shatsthala) journey for salvation as propounded by Saiva agamas (Parameswara Tantra). The first two steps are Bhakta Sthala and Maheswara Sthala which promotes the surrender of ego at the feet of the teacher (Guru). It promotes the practice of morality, ethics, equality, and service to fellow followers & society. It also includes being alert in the present which enables the person to progress along the path which culminates in the union of Jeevatma with Maheswara (Ikya Sthala) (https://en.wikipedia.org/wiki/Shatsthala accessed on 26th June 2021). Prominent saints of this lineage are Lord Basaveswara, Akka Mahadevi, Allam Prabhu & Siddha Rama. The main seats of learning of this school are Srisailam and Varanasi.

Saints of Lingayat School of Saivism from left Basaveswara, Akka Mahadevi and Allam Prabhu

Nadh Saivism: Historically it is denoted by Yoga/Yogi tradition. In modern days it is called Nath Saivism. It has the Adinath (Lord Siva) as the prime Guru. Guru Matsyendra Nadh has popularized it. To have a wider reach, he amalgamated various other schools of Saivism like Kashmiri Saivism, Kaula Saivism, Kapalika Saivism, Pasupata Saivism and even some sects of Buddhism into its fold. It got consolidated as a distinct group of Saivism during Guru Gorakh Nadh who was the direct disciple of Guru Matsyendra Nadh. Guru Gorakh Nadh has instructed the followers to shun tamasic practices derived from Kaula and Kapalika schools and focus more on internalising the energies through Hatha yoga. By the 10th to 11th Century AD, it has spread throughout undivided India including Nepal. It has nine enlightened teachers in its line of Gurus. Both Matsyendra Nath and Gorakh Nadh are from Southern India. However, as part of their spiritual mission, they moved to the Northern parts of India. Nadh tradition has Pan India followers. It tried to erase the castiest (assigning social status to an individual based on his birth) distinctions in society. It is prevalent in parts of Pakistan as well.

Its philosophy regarding the Paramatma, Prakriti and Jeevatma is akin to Kashmiri Saivism. Various Yogic practices which focus on strengthening the body are brought together by this school and promoted as *Hatha Yoga*. It strengthens the body so that the body becomes fit for beholding and comprehending the power of the Almighty. It has 84 special mudras(postures) to cleanse and strengthen the body. The monks of this school lit a sacred fire (Dhuni) at the place where they stay. In the Deccan and parts of south India Guru Dattatreya is associated with this tradition. It has many Sufi saints in its order. Some people believe that Shirdi Saibaba who is generally seen with Dhuni (sacred fire) belong to this lineage.

Guru Dattatreya and Saibaba of Shirdi

Guru Dattatreya and Guru Saibaba line of Nadh Saivism is more popular in the Deccan and other southern regions of India. On the other hand, the Nadh tradition promoted by Gorakhnath is popular in Northern India. It encouraged people to shun caste distinctions and included people from all walks of life in their fold as Nadh Saints. Many Nadh Saints are known for their mystic powers. There are many households Nadhs who practice the Nadh line of Yoga and meditation. Both ascetic and household Nadhs have something in common in their appearance. That is hooped earrings worn through the cartilages of both ears. The second distinct identity is a horn, rudraksha, ring hanging around the neck which is worn on a thread. They blow the horn at daybreak and also after completing the prayer. Jwalamukhi, Haridwar, Gorakhpur, Kadri (in Karnataka), Jogi tilla (Presently in the Punjab province of Pakistan), and Mouli

Nath math (presently in the Sindh Province of Pakistan) are some of their centres of learning. The most popular textual works of this sect are *Siddha Siddhanta Paddhati* & teachings of Gorakh Nadh by the name "Gorakhbani or Goraksha Vachana". All books of Hathayoga have their connection with this tradition.

Guru Matsyendra Nadh and Guru Gorakh Nadh are prominent Gurus of this tradition. As per this school of Saivism, liberation can be attained by consciously ascending the seven levels of worlds made of different degrees of consciousness. They are *Jada jagat* which involves material world including the body which obeys the natural laws, *Prana Jagat* which is beyond the control of normal human being but controls his biological presence, *Mano jagat* which transcends both the Jada jagat and Prana jagat, *Buddhi* jagat which is intellect derived from Satvik Gunas, where better discretion than Mano jagat prevails, *Dharma Jagat* (Satya loka) where universal unchanging everlasting truth behind the creation can be Perceived by Yogi, *Rasa jagat* (Sankshipta Kailasa loka) where the yogi starts beholding the bliss of Divine companionship. Up to this level Prakriti or Mother Goddess Sakti extends her support to Jeevatma and the individual retains consciousness of his own presence. The final loka or abode is *Ananda Jagat (Kailasa or Siva Loka)* where Jeevatma starts beholding the highest state of bliss which is free from qualities bestowed by Prakriti. Jeevatma beholds Lord Siva and acquires his form and qualities. This is called Turiya Anada or the ultimate bliss. Nadh Yogis treat this as the state of Liberation.

Guru Matsyendra Nadh and Guru Gorakh Nadh

To oversee the activities of Nadh followers Akhil Bharatvarshiya Avadhoot Bhesh Barah Panth Yogi Mahasabha situated at Haridwar was established in 1906 and it is active in coordinating more than 500 ashrams/mathas spread across the country. For more information on this sect, refer *Pradee*p Meghawar, 'Thesis on Nath Saivism in Pakistan', Accessed on 9th Aug 2021at https://www.academia.edu/24121327/COMPLETE THESIS pdf?auto=download. Nath Sampradaya by James Mallinson, Available online 'Nadhsampradaya.FP.PDF'

Saiva Siddhanta: It is one of the most ancient schools of Saivism. Like any other Saivitic school it has its origin in Pasupata Saivism. This school also don't believe in the Advaita Philosophy. It promotes Ewaradwaita as that of Srouta Saiva School.

Saints of Saiva Siddhanta (from left) Appar, Gnana Sambadhar, Manikvachakar

This school of Saivitic thought proposes that the Paramatma is present in both Prakriti and Jeevatma. Paramatma is the Soul of the Jeevatma. Jeevatma can't have an independent existence. It has to either, remain in ignorant association with Prakriti or in a state of wakeful consciousness of Paramatma. Jeevatma has acquired the quality of Self-knowledge (Sentiency) from Paramatma who is Soul within the Jeevatma. Senses and mind which are born out of Prakriti can't realize the true nature of the Jeevatma or Paramatma as the Prakriti in insentient. The soul can either have the consciousness of Prakriti or Paramatma but not both at a time. **Prakriti is the Law of causation** appointed by Paramatma, which acts as an instrument for the evolution of Jeevatma. Prakriti attracts the Jeevatma with her infinite attractions, but finally tires it. This makes the Jeevatma understand the fallacy of indulging in the colours of

122

Prakriti. As per this school, there are 36 attributes which assist the Jeevatma in its evolution, 24 of which are part of Prakriti which were already elaborated as part of the Sankhya school. The remaining 12 attributes proposed by this school are elaborated below.

Samaya, Niyati, Kala, Vidya, Raga, Purusha, and Maya forms the attributes from the 25th to 31. Samaya is a measure of the past, allows feelings in present, and contains something in store for the future. It is a bridge between the present and the future. Niyati fixes the sequence or Karma (action). Kala induces action. Intelligence is induced by Vidya. Purush induces perception through the senses. Maya induces ignorance. Attributes (Tatvas) up to 31 are more material in nature. Attributes from 32nd to 36 are pure tattvas which are completely free from Prakriti. They are Suddha Vidya, Iswara tatva, Sadasiva tatva, Sakti tatva and Sivatva. Sakti tattva induces action, Sadasiva tattva induces action and knowledge in equal proportions, and Sivatva induces Knowledge alone. Liberation involves experiencing the Sivatva.

Sakta School of Thought: Sakta school is generally viewed in conjunction with Saivitic schools. Sakti or the Mother Goddess Prakriti is essential to give expressive form to the Divine wisdom. Sakta school believes that whatever we can see, feel, and comprehend is Sakti. Siva cannot manifest without Sakti.

Sri Vidya (The crown of the jewel of wisdom), and Dasa Maha Vidyas (Ten Ultimate Forms of Prakritic Wisdom) are some of the practices through which the learned teachers of this school invoke and behold the

Sakti. Dasa Maha vidyas are Kali, Bhuvaneswari, Chinnamasta, Bhagala Mukhi, Matangi, Sodasi, Dhumavati, Tripura Sundari, Tara, Bhairavi. These forms have significant inner meanings. Though it is difficult and out of context to give subtle meaning behind each of these forms, a typical explanation of 'Kali' which is one of the ten forms of Sakti is given briefly below.

Kali represents the highest conscious force which is ferocious towards demonic aspects of the human mind. She can unroot the demonic energies without a trace. The Chamunda (Chamundeshwari) form of Kali represents the ability of Kali, to crush all the wavering thoughts and ever-branching thoughts of human minds. The uprooting of the demon 'Raktabeeja' who was known to have the ability to recreate himself from each drop of blood that falls from his body onto the ground indicates the ability of the human mind that projects out endless branches of thoughts from each thought. The ability of Sakti to uproot such a demon indicates, her ability to subdue the human mind which takes branches and subbranches. Thus, Sakti in the form of Kali can crush the wavering nature of the mind. Deep philosophical meanings of the various forms of Dasa Maha Vidyas are not supposed to be described in public discourse. It should be learned from a learned teacher.

Goddess Annapurna (Nourishing facet of Prakriti) and Goddess Kali (Dissolving Facets of Prakriti)

As per the Sakta Agamas, the visible world is a wave (lower Prakriti of Sakti) created in the otherwise stagnant Siva. Since Siva is infinite and all-encompassing, he doesn't have the feeling of 'I' (Aham in Sanskrit) ness. Since to have the "I" ness there should be something other than Siva. From Siva, Sakti came out as a wave having the ability to self-recognise itself and also made Lord Siva recognise himself. Hence for Siva to manifest, Sakti is essential. As per this school, Siva needs Sakti not only to manifest but also to act.

Without Sakti, Siva is infinite, comprehensive yet equivalent to null. This is close to the Mahasunya concept of Veerasaiva, or the Suddha Chaitanya of Dwaita. The wave or the disturbance denoted as Sakti is also called 'Samvit'. However, it is not the highest truth as that of Siva who is beyond the reach of Prakritic tools. Samvit is the truth which can express itself independently. Samvit has two facets as per the Sakta School. They are Creative Samvit (Srujantmaka or Upper Prakriti as per Bhagavad Gita) and Dissolutive (Layatmaka or lower Prakriti as per Bhagavad Gita). At the beginning of the creation, from Siva who doesn't have the feeling of "I" ness, the upper Prakriti brings out a part of Siva with "I" ness feeling and introduces it in the womb of lower Prakriti. These seeds are the individual Jeevatmas which come under the influence of three primitive qualities of lower Prakriti (Satvik, Rajasik and Tamasik) kickstarting the long journey of evolution. At the start of the creation, the differentiated form of Prakriti (lower Prakriti) throws the veil of Maya or nest on the Jeevatmas and at the end of creation lower Prakriti dissolves into upper Prakriti. The lower Prakritic aspect reprecipitates again at the beginning of the next cycle of creation. Thus, Sakti is the main driver of creation whereas the Siva is above the cycles of creation and dissolution. Some scholars of this school believe that the wave that got triggered in Siva bringing the differentiation in otherwise static and complete Siva is 'Kala' (Time). (Kala means one which counts. Siva is Maha Kala and Sakti which triggered the Kala is Maha Kali).

The human body carries both the Siva and Sakti. The spark of Siva is present in the body in the Dahara Akasha (the emptiness present in the Jeevatma). Spark of Sakti is present as Kundalini. However, Sakti is present in the dormant form. By meditative contemplation, it can be invoked. As Sakti ascends towards the abode of Siva, it dissolves lower Prakritic elements of the body. As long as Kundalini is not invoked in the body, the body is like a corpse for the upper Prakritic world and alive in the lower Prakritic world. Once it is invoked it attains the Sivatva (the original form of Lord Siva), which enables the Jeevatma to behold its true nature. Sri Vidya Upasana (meditating on either of the ten forms of Goddess), and Lalita Upasana (mediating on Goddess Lalita) are popular sub schools of this line of Hindu practice. Mystic symbol which depicts the origin of the universe from a Bindu (dot) and then spreading with the vital energies of Siva (depicted with upward triangles) and Sakti (depicted with downward triangles) are used by the practitioners of this school to meditate upon the secrets of the creation and to withdraw the mind from the outer realms. Great Proponents of this school were Gowda Pada (Guru of Adi Sankara), Somananda, Abhinava Gupta and Bhaskara Raya.

Holy grain (Paramatma) multiplies itself into three Primitive Realities (Paramatma, Prakriti and Jeevatma). (Gita XIV:3). Paramatma and Prakriti further multiply their manifestation (Gita XIV:4)

The above image is also called Srichakra which is present in almost all Sakti temples. It is believed that the actual life force of the idol of Sakti is present in this Srichakra, and the idol we see in the temple is a physical representation of the Sakti present in Srichakra.

Other forms of Goddesses of the Sakta line like Tripura Sundari, and Bhairavi are having strong links with the Saivitic yogic traditions especially Srouta Saiva and Kashmiri Saivitic tradition. Deeper meanings of these forms need to be understood from learned Yogis of these schools. Especially Upasana of Bala Tripurasundari (The meditative technique to behold Sakti as an eight-year-old girl) is prevalent among Srouta Saiva followers and the Upasana of Bharavi is prevalent among Kashmiri Saivitic followers.

Saura (Sun) School: This school believes that Paramatma is an infinite glow. It has parity with the glow of the Sun. He glows like thousands of Suns glowing at a time (Gita XI:12). The way Jeevatma imparts life force to the body, Paramatma imparts life force to the universe. Sun has parity with Paramatma as he imparts life force to the creation around him. The infinite glow of Paramatma is all-pervading which is not visible to our eyes, however, the glow of the Sun is a visible manifestation of the glow of Paramatma. Paramatma is the light of all lights including the glow of the Sun (Gita XV:6, Kathopanishad 2.2.15). Thus for the realm in which we are living Paramatma's visible attribute that we can feel is Sun. He is the light of all lights that we can experience. He is the ultimate glow, He is the ultimate truth and all-pervading (Rigveda, Maha Saura Mantra 56-58). Sun God referred to in Vedas is not confined to the Sun that is visible to the naked eye. Sun God is all-pervading Paramatma. However, he projected his flag in the sky as the Sun we see in our solar system. Thus, to guide us towards eternal truth, to dispel our ignorance and to sustain the creation, Paramatma projected himself from the darkness as Sun (Mahasaura Mantra, Rigveda). He is supervising the nourishment of the Jeevatmas (Gita XV:12,13). Besides manifesting externally as Sun, he is present in the body as digestive fire thus supervising the nourishment of each cell of the body (Gita XV:14). Readers have to understand that Sun worship is not mere worship of the visible Sun in the sky. It is the exploration of the infinite all-pervading light. That infinite Paramatma has all attributes of the visible Sun. The way the Sun in the sky is the sustainer of life on this earth yet he is not touched by the life on the earth, Paramatma is the source of all Jeevatmas. Similar to the fact that the body is illuminated by Jeevatma, the Sun God is illuminating the Universe as the Soul of the Universe (Rigveda: 1:115-1).

Like a Swan flying in the clear skies, Sun God is present as Paramatma in the body. He is the sacred fire lit in the Vedic rituals; he is the digestive fire in the body. He is the flag projecting out as Sun from the infinite truth. I am offering my salutations to it. Let my intellect blossom with his blessings (Maha Saura Mantra from Rigveda).

The seeds for the Advaita Philosophy are present in the Brihadaranyaka Upanishad. This Upanishad is believed to be told by Seer Yagna Valka to his wife Maitreyi. Seer Yagna Valka received Vedic knowledge from the Sun God. He Propagated Shukla Yajurveda and is believed to be the earliest proponent of Advaita Philosophy. Thus, the Saura school falls under the Advaita line of thought. It emphasizes identifying the Jeevatma as the light within the body, which is lighting up the body like the Sun is lighting up the whole world (Gita XIII: 18, V:24). Praying visible Sun God is praying Paramatma himself. It is like beholding one of the visible attributes of Paramatma as a rope to climb to his abode. Patanjali Yoga Sutras contain the mystic practice of focusing on the Sun (Chapter III:26). This practice can enable the seeker to visualize various Divine realms (seven upper worlds where the enlightened souls live and seven lower worlds where those souls live whose Karmic aggregate does not fit to find a place on earth or the worlds further above). Many Hindu practices are linked to the concept of invoking the power of the Sun God or his intense ability to dispel the darkness. Lord Rama is said to have worshipped the Sun God and invoked the required Divine power to conquer Ravana. Chhath Puja festival popular in north India and Ratha Saptami festival popular in Southern parts of India are related to 'Saura School'.

Hey Sun God, Bless us with noble thoughts, noble intellect, and noble vision. Bless us with noble children, Bless us to have good health, and Keep us away from sinful thoughts and actions. Bless us with long life so that we can see you and salute you every day for a long time (Maha Saura Mantra:44, Rigveda)

Kumara worship (Worshippers of Son of Siva): It is one of the six authentic branches of Hinduism approved by Vedas and Upanishads. Karthikeya, Subrahmanya, and Murugan are other names of Kumara. The birth of the Son of Siva is known to be from the seed of Siva which descended and was nurtured by Mother Goddesses (Krittikas). Those who understand the Sankhya school of thought and the Genesis given in the previous chapters can better correlate the inner meanings behind the origin of Kumara. The concept of 'Kumara (Son)' evolving into an equivalent being as that of the Supreme God himself is an extension of the concept of the Sankhya school. It is the promotion of Jeevatma to a state where it is equivalent to Paramatma in its attributes and vastness (Refer to Sankhya Philosophy for further understanding). As the Sankhya school has strong connections with Saivitic and Sakta schools, the worship of Kumara is also intertwined with these two schools of thought. Kumara has relevance to Yogic traditions which believe in the six subtle energy centres spread along the base of the spine to the brain in the body.

"With eyes steadied between the eye brows, having freed from worldly objects, with life force being awakened from its dormant state and drawn up to the mid-point of eyes, the

seeker reaches a level where he is absorbed in inner bliss. He relishes in the inner light & learns to relax in the company of illuminating Paramatma present within. Such an Individual becomes one with Paramatma (Gita V:24,27,28)".

It is believed by Yogis of the Saivitic line that the life force of human beings (Energy of Jeevatma) is in a dormant state like a snake coiled and resting. With the practice of austerities of self-control, kindness, unselfishness, & meditative contemplation the life force starts raising through the spine crossing the six subtle energy centres during its journey. When it reaches the subtle centre called 'Sahasrara (thousand petal flower)' it merges with the Maheswara who is seated there (Gita XV:16). Sahasrara is also referred to as Kutastha (Gita VI;8). Kutastha means a junction where all sorts of Prakritic inclinations (Vikaras in Sanskrit) merge and comes to standstill. Seating at 'Kutastha' Maheswara foresees the activities of Jeevatma. Every memory that sparks in our mind, each piece of knowledge that we acquire, even the loss of memory or misinterpretation made by the Jeevatma is being observed by Maheswara (Gita XV:15). Thus, there are two Purushas. One is the Maheswara seated at Sahasrara which is on the top of the spine and the other one is the Kumara who is generally present in the form of dormant coiled force at the bottom of the spine. The lower purusha or Kumara losses identity in a cyclic manner during the death. On the other hand, higher Purusha (Maheswara seated in the Kutastha) retains identity in an uninterrupted manner (Gita XV:16). Kumara ascends the subtle centres of consciousness like a serpentine crawling up the path reaching Kutastha Maheswara. At this stage, Kumara finds equilibrium with the Maheswara (Gita VI:8).

Every individual carries a split personality till he conquers Kutastha (Gita VI:34). This is because the natural self of Jeevatma inclines to move towards Maheswara on the other hand the pull of mind & senses makes the consciousness outward. When the individual's consciousness takes flight from hiding below the spine to the Kutastha, then he attains salvation. At this stage, the split personality vanishes as the Jeevatma has reached its ultimate abode where it enjoys the eternal joy and company of the Paramatma (Gita VI:8,10 XV:16). Thus, the journey of Kumara (Son of God) completes.

Readers can correlate now the prayers offered to the Snake God in Hindu practice as an invocation of Kundalini within. Readers also can correlate offering the milk at the snake's hills to appease the snake God. It is like pouring in the Satvik qualities (Gita VI: 5-8), to trigger the raise of Kumara within us. In the Vedic literature, Kumara has parity with the worship of light or Agni. The Vedic hymns which hail Lord Agni are the hymns for invoking the spark within the body to burn the Karmic bondage.

The Ganapatya: This is one of the six authentic branches of Hinduism having derived its authenticity from the Vedas and Upanishads. Ganapati refers to the "Head of a Group". Ganapati refers to the Subtle Divine sound "OM" which is the head of a group of Divine powers. OM precedes every set of Divine hymns. It is this subtle sound which opens the door to the realms of Divinity (Gita VIII:13). The Physical form of Ganapati that we see is the physical manifestation of the Divine subtle sound 'OM'.

We invoke the chief leader of heavenly beings. He is the sacred Ganapati. We invoke him to dispel the evil forces and obstructions. Those who come under his protection will never experience sorrow. He will drive away all harms from his devotees (Rigveda.2.23.1/2/5).

Rigveda hails the Ganapati as the Protector of the Vedic hymns. It invokes Ganapati as the King of Vedic hymns who protects and preserves the Vedas (Rugveda 2.23.1). He is the wisdom in the wise, poetic quality of the poets. In the Yogic line, it is believed that there are six subtle energy centres along the base of the spine to the Sahasrara. Each of these six energy centres is presided over by a Divine force. First among the six energy centres is the Muladhara chakra (the root centre of energy) present at the base of the spine. It is believed that Lord Ganapati is the presiding deity for this centre. The upward movement of the life force of any individual should start from the place where the Lord Ganapati is the presiding deity. Hence it is believed that without the blessings of the Ganapati, the spiritual journey will not move forward.

Goddess Gayatri: The Repository of Vedic Wisdom and the Unifying force of Hindu Thought:

We meditate to behold the highest truth OM. It is the omniscient Divine from which everything springs out and dissolves back. Let this noble truth enrich our intellect (Rigveda 3.62.10).

As described earlier, there are six basic sects of the Hindu faith which have derived their authenticity from the Vedas and Upanishads. They are Saiva, Vaishnava, Sakta, Saura, Ganapatya, Skanda/Kumara. Either of these paths will lead to the same destination. Since it is difficult to comprehend the entire essence of all these six paths enumerated by Vedas by any individual, Bhagavad Gita proclaimed complete surrender at the feet of the almighty as one of the simple methods to attain liberation (Gita XVIII:66). Hymns towards Goddess Gayatri, in essence, are an ardent appeal to Almighty to grace us and enlighten us with the wisdom required to behold the ultimate truth (Rigveda 3.62.10). Goddess Gayatri is the personification of the entire wisdom of Vedas. Vedas pronounced the six basic sects or paths. Worship of Gayatri is an integrated way of invoking all six paths of wisdom. It is made compulsory for every devout Hindu to bow before her every morning which means bowing before the Vedic wisdom. Goddess Gayatri is a reminder to everyone that, these six paths are not different from each other. One should not treat any of these paths as inferior. For general information of the reader, Gayatri is a meter or style of Sanskrit poetry used in this hymn (Mantra). Savita is the Presiding deity of the hymn. Sun God is treated as the visible manifestation of Savita's energy.

Sikhism: This tradition was initiated by Guru Nanak. It has nine Gurus in its line. The last among the line of Gurus is Guru Gobind Singh. Gurus of this lineage brought out noble teachings in the form of devotional songs which are having the power to touch the soul. They were written by God's realized souls in the Divine ecstasy. As per this tradition Sat (the truth) is ultimate and practising it honestly (Sadachara) is the ultimate path. Gurus of this tradition suggested seekers be conscious of the *Value* and *Purpose* of the work being taken up. Instead of focusing on the activities that can give temporary value, one should focus on activities that bring permanent Divine transformation.

Sikh Gurus: Guru Nanak Dev and Guru Gobind Singh

As per this tradition, there is one ultimate truth. That is the 'OM'. It is eternal, all-pervading, above the limitations of time. With the blessings of Guru, the true nature of the ultimate truth can be known. Views of Sikhism on Prakriti, Jeevatma and Liberation are briefly given below.

The creation is cyclic. There are times where there is nothing else existed other than Paramatma. At the beginning of creation, he created Prakriti and the three basic qualities of Satvik, Rajasik, and Tamasik. He also created Devas (celestial beings) and Asuras. Paramatma created Purusha and instated him to oversee the play. Thus, Paramatma is Parama Purusha (one who is above the Purusha and Prakriti). The light of Paramatma is lighting up everything in this universe. Paramatma is omnipresent and omnipotent.

Jeevatmas are the waves that appeared in the infinite ocean of Paramatma. They raise from Paramatma at his will. They are not separate from Paramatma. Thus, every Jeevatma or every living being is having the spark of Paramatma. But when the Jeevatma forgets its true self and inculcates 'I' ness (Aham), it falls into the infinite cycle of life and death. Guru has the power to heal the Jeevatma and remind us of the truth. Sikh Gurus don't believe in the Avatara (Paramatma descending himself on earth). They believe that Paramatma sends evolved souls to earth to guide struggling mankind. Paramatma himself never descends on earth. As per this tradition, there is a difference between the Guru and Paramatma. Guru is the one who knows how to surrender to Paramatma. Sikhism also emphasized following the teaching of the Guru with full faith. This tradition enlightens the seekers not to see the Guru as a body, but rather as the one whom the Paramatma has chosen to convey his Divine message. Thus, Sikhism emphasizes giving priority to the teachings of the Guru and the message he has given rather than involving in the idolatry of the Guru. One who follows the teachings of the Guru can get liberated from the cycle of life and death as the teachings of the Guru have the power to break Karmic bondage. This is because the teachings of the Guru are the message of Paramatma sent to humans. Sikhism also doesn't believe in Sanyasa (renunciation). Rather it emphasizes earning the needs of the body and then sharing the remaining with other needy people. It promotes donations for the benefit of the needy.

Singing the Guru's message in Divine ecstasy is a popular practice of this line.

Sikhism doesn't believe in Mayavada or the concept of believing Prakriti is a delusion. As per this tradition, Paramatma is true and his creation is also true. Nothing in this universe is a delusion. We are not dreaming of anything. What you are seeing is real. Through Sadachara (Good conduct), that is through the practice of honesty, through donating to the needy, through following the Guru's message one can attain a state where the Divinity of Almighty will descend on him. He will be liberated from the karmic bonds. In the liberated state, Jeevatma identifies its unity with the Almighty and dissolves itself in him thus slowly losing its own identity. Thus, in terms of the concept of liberation, it has similarities with the Advaita philosophy.

Buddhism: Buddhism is also a prominent Philosophical path of India. Buddhist philosophy encompasses the parts of Shat Darshana (Six Schools of Indian Philosophy) especially Tarka and Vaiseshika schools but is not confined itself to completely fit into them. As per Buddhist thought, there is no ultimate and eternal Purusha or Soul. Buddhism takes the analogy of fire and wood. As per this analogy, there can't be fire without wood, similarly, there is no possibility of the existence of independent consciousness without the object. On the other hand, Sankhya, Yoga and the Mimamsa schools say that even when the Jeevatma ceases its connections with the matter, still it retains pure consciousness that is conscious of itself (Patanjali Yoga Sutras Chapter I:3). Buddhism emphasized more on following the path of righteousness (Dharma), the path of non-violence, the path of Buddha with less emphasis on Jeevatma and Paramatma.

Lord Buddha and Lord Mahavira

Jainism: It is one of the oldest schools of Philosophy dating back to the prehistoric period. It has twenty-four enlightened Gurus in its line of seers starting from Rishabha Nadha and ending with Mahaveera. Its emphasis on the practice of nonviolence and its philosophical thought on 'non-absolutism (Anekatva)' made it a distinct religious thought. Absolutism proposes the Almighty as one single immutable truth (Advaita) whereas non-absolutism proposes that, the ultimate truth is infinite, and its modes of existence cannot be comprehended in its totality by finite human perception. Only *'Kevalins'* (omniscient beings) can comprehend it. So, the knowledge that can be available or that can be explained is not the ultimate knowledge, rather at the best it can be a partial truth. The story of six blind men and an elephant can best explain the truth that one perceives with his limited knowledge. Thus, Jainism promoted an open mind to accommodate all other philosophical thoughts.

Jainism classified various living beings based on the degree of sensual perception they carry. Among various beings, humans are at the top of the hierarchy with five sensual organs and intellect as the sixth one distinguishing them from other beings. Jainism believes in the "Law of Karma". However, Jainism further differentiated various Karmas (activities) into two categories namely Dravya Karmas (involving body) and Bhava Karma (involving intellect and thoughts). The former can influence one's body & subtle body, whereas the latter influences the intellect. Dravya Karma and Bhava Karma together pull the Jeevatma towards the suitable abode. The only way to salvation for Jeevatma is to purify the Bhava Karma through austerities (Tapas). Austerities are possible for humans only. Thus, humans are above even celestial beings as celestial beings can't perform Tapasya or Austerities. Thus, humans are much nearer to Salvation than celestial beings. Thus, Jainism differs from other conventional Vedic schools which upheld the concept that Celestial beings are more advanced than humans in their quest for liberation. It also differs in its approach in accepting what constitutes direct evidence. Vedantic schools identify one which is perceived through senses as direct evidence. However, Jainism doesn't believe in direct evidence derived from the senses or mind. It only recognizes the Yogic vision (Atma Drishti) as direct evidence and rest all sensory-based experiences as partial evidence. Thus, Jainism differed from Nyaya and Vaiseshika schools. Only when the individual reaches a state of experiencing and beholding the truth without being mediated through sensory tools and mind, then he reaches a state of Pure Knowledge (Kevala Gnana) where he can comprehend the truth (Almighty) in its totality. In such a state, Jeevatma possesses infinite knowledge, infinite perception, infinite happiness and infinite energy. In this state, Jeevatma enjoys the blissful company of Paramatma.

Till that stage, everything known is partial or incomplete (Syadvada). To reach such a state, as an essential first step, the individual has to purify himself or herself through five essential practices. They are non-violence (Ahimsa), Truth (Satya), non-stealing (asteya), being celibate (Brahmacharya) & not owning or possessing others hard earned things (aparigraha).

Non-violence is the foremost among the five essential practices of Jainism. For instance, the truth which ensures peace & harmony only is the real truth. Anything truth which will deviate from nonviolence, that is the truth that brings suffering to others can't be truth, though it is a fact. Nonviolence includes not only being nonviolent physically, but it also includes being nonviolent in thoughts as well. Nonviolence should be practised unconditionally. Even when the enemy is inflicting injury, one should bear it with nonviolent thoughts. Such a high degree of nonviolence coupled with emphasis on truth could bring miracles and make the enemies into friends and thus the entire world will be filled with peace.

Jain scriptures have many stories of Jian monks who practised such a high degree of truth and nonviolent attitude even when they were suffering at the hands of violent people. It is well known that, Mahatma Gandhi derived his strong faith in the power of nonviolence and truth not only from Bhagavad Gita but also from the Jain tradition. Everyone knows results of 'Satyagraha' promoted by Mahatma Gandhi.

The Celestial Sound "OM" as the Unifying Platform: As discussed, Indian Philosophy has many branches. It allowed every facet of human exploration to find the truth as long as it has not deviated from Sadachara (Noble thoughts, Noble activities). From the perspective of Sastras (Scriptures), the common root for all branches is 'Shat Darshanas' or the six orthodox schools of Indian Philosophy.

OM is the Ultimate Divine Form, it is everything that was, is and will be. All other things which transcend time are also

OM (Mandyuka Upanishad). It is the fountain from where Vedas, Consciousness & Wisdom spring up. It is the ultimate abode for Jeevatma to reach (Gita XVII:23, Gita VIII:13).

All religious thoughts evolved in this sacred land derived their basics from the six orthodox schools for logical extrapolation of spiritual thoughts. These six schools of thought have become the platform and defined the boundaries for spiritual debate between various schools of religious thought over the centuries.

Though Indian Philosophical schools differed in their beliefs, all the religious schools that evolved in scared land of India have a commonality in accepting the Supremacy of "OM'. As per the Bhagavad Gita "OM" is the ultimate destiny for the Purusha (Jeevatma). If anyone leaves the body while chanting "OM" with the mind fixed on the Paramatma, his soul will get elevated to the ultimate celestial plane where the cycle of birth and death can't reach (Gita VIII:13). Chanting OM while leaving the body can't happen if Sadachara or Yoga is not practised while the life force is present in its full splendour in the body. It is possible only for those who through the practice of Yoga mastered the art of withdrawing the life force from all senses, and guiding it towards the Sahasrara (a thousand-petal Divine flower which connects the Atman with Paramatma like Lord Brahma is connected to Lord Vishnu) (Gita VIII:12,13). To attain such a state of perfection many seekers renounce everything during their lifetime and explore the secrets of Yoga (Gita

146

VIII: 11). OM is also known as the Akshara and meditation on OM is called Aksharopasana. It is the highest form of Upasana or religious practice as suggested by Upanishads (Kathopanishad II: 15-17). One who beholds "OM" realizes the Almighty as "OM". Brahma loka is also referred to as **Akshardham** in Upanishads. This is the ultimate plane for the soul to reach. It stays there in eternal bliss (Gita VIII:16). This Aksharadham is the source of all shining life present in all other realms of the universe (Katha Upanishad V:15). It may seem difficult to attain such a state. But Lord says in Bhagavad Gita, that " it is very easy to reach such a realm for those who through steadfast devotion surrendered themselves to me (Paramatma) and acted every moment of life with consciousness my omnipresence (Gita VIII:14)".

To make the practice of Akshara Upasana simple and continuous, Mantras were introduced by sages. They are celestial sounds having special powers. Each mantra is preceded by "OM'. Among various mantras, Gayatri Mantra is considered the ultimate Mantra which seekers of various schools of Hindu Philosophy practice daily. This mantra involves reciting "OM" and seeking Divine blessings to enrich our intellect to behold the ultimate truth. Goddess Gayatri is a personified form of OM and Vedic wisdom. Each of the religious sects of Hinduism has its own sacred mantra for recitation, but each of them starts with OM. Thus, OM is the source that shines all facets of Indian thought.

In Jainism 'OM' is considered as a condensed form of reference to Pancha Parameshti or the five supreme beings. It represents five levels of

147

religious authority worthy of veneration. In Buddhism 'OM' is identified with the sound of the universe. It constitutes an important part of many Buddhist mantras (chants). 'OM' is the part of mula mantra (central and highest chants) of Sikhism. Thus sacred 'OM' is the unifying force of religious thoughts that evolved in India.

Concluding Remarks: Paramatma, Purusha (Jeevatma) and Prakriti are three entities of the universe which are identified as the Divine Trinity. Liberation (Moksha) of the Jeevatma from the Prakriti and reaching the abode of Paramatma is the ultimate result of the right spiritual practice. Though all schools of Hindu thought accept the existence of the Divine Trinity, there is a subtle difference in their interpretation of attributes of Prakriti (the reality of the material world vs illusion) and the state of Moksha. This debate led to the formation of many branches in Hinduism. However, all these branches are confined to the boundaries of Shat Darshanas (six orthodox schools of Hindu Philosophy) for their debate with other sects. Bhagavad Gita accepted the existence of Anekatva (innumerable facets of Godhood) yet stressed that all these facets in fact derive their shine from the single source that is OM. This ultimate source can be reached through any satvik (truth and compassion) practice of spirituality.

"In whatever the form the Devotee worships me, I bless him in that form thus making his faith stronger (Gita VII:21,22). Any Satvik (truthful and compassionate) path whether it be Sankhya,

Karma Yoga, or Bhakti Yoga when practised properly will lead the individual to my abode (Gita V:4,5)".

Readers are advised to understand that the ancient sages perceived the Almighty in different forms at different points in time. It was graceful when sages sought wisdom (like Dakshina Murty) and it was fierce when protection from the wicked was sought (Goddess Kali).

Having known various schools of thought one has to understand that, no school of thought can help the individual to reach the abode of Almighty if he has not overcome the three primitive qualities namely Satvik, Rajasik and Tamasik (Gita XIV:20). After overcoming the primitive qualities, the individual soul realizes the true nature of itself and starts looking towards the Paramatma who is accompanying the journey (Gita XIII:23). Once it learns the art of looking back towards the almighty, then it need not take any more physical forms, as it doesn't need the assistance of mother nature (Prakriti) anymore. It submerges itself in the vastness of the super soul (Gita XIII:24,25). In subsequent chapters methods to overcome primitive qualities through the path of Dharma (righteousness) and meditative contemplation are discussed.

Chapter V

The Austerity of Senses and Right Association

Prelude: The essence of austerities of senses (Indriya Tapa) is to use them for the right cause. When senses are controlled, the intellect of the individual blossoms (Gita II: 61). One has to understand that, the austerities of senses never promote inaction, rather, it pitches for the right use of senses for the upliftment of self and society. It also pitches for strengthening control of mind over senses, so that, senses can be withdrawn at will when the need arises (Gita II:58). Right use of senses is the 'Austerities of Senses'. It does not stop at physical abstinence. It encompasses overcoming the longing for sensual pleasures. Without succeeding in the austerities of senses, no one can succeed in the physical or spiritual world (Gita II: 68).

Jeevatma rides the chariot of body drawn by senses (Gita XV:10). When the individual invokes the Divinity, it guides

the senses and makes senses as tools for success (Gita II.61).
One who fails to invoke the Divine intellect losses course and
perishes (Gita II: 62,63).

Reasons for Misuse of Senses: The mind is the master of the senses. In general, most of the people who have fallen in their life are those whose mind has accepted the senses as its master. The senses of such persons eclipse the power of discrimination. This results in the loss of the course of the lifeboat (Gita II:67).

Senses are not easy to tame. They try to violently overpower even those who are making sincere efforts to tame them (Gita II:60). This happens due to goalless effort. Those who don't have defined goals and those who don't have the ambition to progress towards the goal become easy prey for the senses. The goal of life need not be spiritual, it can be any progressive and positive goal which can uplift us. However, pursuing the goal through Dharmic means is essential. It can't happen without bringing the senses under the control.

The victory of the senses over mind or mind over senses will not happen in a single day. It involves a great tussle between these two. Where the senses win over the mind, the sequence of their victory is as follows (Gita II:62,63).

In the first stage of degradation, the individual develops the following traits.

• Attachment with certain objects which entertain the senses,

• Desire to possess those objects,

• Desire to satisfy the ego

Till this point, the mind will be in a state of dilemma on which path to be chosen, the path shown by senses, or the path shown by the discriminative intellect. If the mind chooses the former, then the person enters the next level of self-ruining, which involves

• Frustration over the circumstances.

• Loss of discrimination borne out of frustration and anger. Senses snatch the mind completely from the intellect,

• Loss of course of life as the mind got enslaved to senses. Mind starts working only for sensual pleasures or ego satisfaction thus ruining the individual's life completely.

A person with the mind enslaved to senses can never experience peace in life. He losses the course of his journey (Gita II:66,67). Thus, robbed of discrimination, such a person will not only act as an enemy to himself but also acts as an enemy to his associates and society at large.

Out of many qualities that the mind can dwell some are identified as the most dangerous. All those who wish to prosper in life should know them and should make a conscious effort to keep away from them. Such dangerous qualities are listed below.

Most Dangerous Sensual Qualities and Methods to Prune Them: Lust, hatred, and greediness are the most dangerous qualities that can ruin life (Gita XVI:21). It is to be understood that at birth, six enemies in the form of basic instincts get attached with every human being. They are **Lust, anger, greed, pride, false identity & jealousy**. If they are not pruned properly, they overgrow and ruin the intellect. Even the most learned people fail to prune their basic instincts. As a result, they lose socially, economically, and spiritually.

Arjuna asked the questions that arise in every seeker. *He asked, what is that force that is instigating humans to indulge in sinful acts?* How the senses rob the discretion and forcefully position the individual in sinful acts (Gita III:36). Lord Krishna Answered

• Rajo guna (the urge to act) when got mixed with lust, anger and greediness makes the individual vulnerable to coming under the control of the senses leading to indulgence in sinful acts. (Gita III:37,38,39).

• When the mind is polluted with unnatural attachment or aversion towards certain objects then senses can act as robbers who rob the discriminative power of the mind leading to indulgence in non-dharmic acts (Gita III:34)

Lord Krishna said that the mind (Manah) is above senses, intellect (Buddhi) is above the mind and above the intellect, there is the Soul (Gita III:43). To win over the senses one must be conscious of the Soul present in the body and should start identifying self as Soul rather than a mere body. One who practices it firmly, can win the basic instincts of lust, anger, and greediness (Gita III:49). However, such a level of progress cannot be attained overnight. Hence, Lord Krishna has given many other suggestions to progress in the path of Self - realization. They are elaborated on below.

Right Association / Divine Friendship: See whether you are in the right association?, if not search for such an association. It can be physical in the form of *Satsang (a Group of people yearning for peace through the synergy of noble thoughts)*. How to recognize the right association or right friend is given below.

With their minds fixed on Paramatma, with their senses absorbed completely in Divine service, they enlighten each other. They are absorbed in Divine bliss. They are delighted in each other's company (Gita X:9). Those who seek such company are assured of Divine grace (Gita X:10)

A right friend should have purity of thought, steadfastness in improving knowledge, ready to donate some resources (money, time etc.—) to the needy.

He should be upright, should have no intention to harm anyone (non-violent in thoughts and actions), compassionate towards all beings, should not have a fickle mind, should not have the habit of finding fault in others, should not have the intention to own property of others, should have control over his anger, should be free from false pride, should have forbearance, should not be envious at other's progress. Above all he should have a strong resolve to imbibe noble qualities in life (Gita XVI:1-3). It may be difficult to find a friend or association with all such qualities. Hence it is often advised to study the scriptures to invoke Divine friendship with the likes of Lord Rama, Hanuman, Lord Siva or great sages, seers, and dwell on their qualities. By invoking these Divine personalities, we can invoke similar Divine qualities within us. Feel their presence in day-to-day life, and consult them spiritually at every moment of your life's journey. The soul within will receive the Divine guidance. If earnestly sought, Almighty will become our friend, master, path and goal (Gita IX:18). One who invokes such a friend or association will never get deviated from the path of Dharma and from the path of success.

In the physical world, it is difficult to find any individual with all the above-listed qualities. However, if some of the qualities like being truthful, nonviolent, compassionate etc.— are overwhelmingly present in an individual, understand that, it is part of the Divine glory manifesting. Accept the person as your mentor and continue to associate (Gita X:41).

Wrong Associations/ Perverted Friendship (Gita XVI:7-11,14): It is essential to know what kind of people or associations are to be avoided.

• Keep away from those who harbour the qualities of untruthfulness, arrogance, harsh attitude, getting emotionally agitated frequently (anxiety), attitude to deceive others (deceitful), and having no intention to improve their knowledge yet carry a feeling of knowing everything.

• Keep away from people who don't have clarity in their thoughts and deeds, and possess poor discrimination between what is to be done and what is not to be done.

• Keep away from those who do not have faith in the Law of Karma and the existence of Divine power.

• Keep away from people who believe that the creation originated out of lust between the opposite sex.

• Keep away from those who don't have any other aim than, satisfying their senses with endless lust, desires & evil ideas.

• Keep away from those who don't have an open mind to accommodate others' ideas, thoughts, and faiths.

• Keep away from those polluted minds, who are ready to go to the extent of physically attacking or slaying people of other faiths or philosophies.

Such perverted people themselves become one with hell and destruction. Persons who associate with such friends will ruin themselves. Societies which promote such qualities create hell and will slide into that hell (Gita XVI:16, Gita IX:.25). Any sort of association with them either personal (Friendship with such persons) or impersonal (reading such books, watching, or listening to contents which promote such ideas) is a self-ruining act.

However, one should not keep away from such people out of hatred. Have compassion towards all such people. Wish their recovery towards the right attitude (Gita V: 25, VI:9). Look for every opportunity to uplift such people from ignorance.

Result of Friendship or Association: Understand that those who choose friends or associations with the qualities mentioned under the Divine friendship not only proposer in their life but also seed prosperity in many others' lives. They can reach the highest echelons of human life.

On the same note, those who imbibe any of the qualities listed under the perverted friends will get ruined. The degree of ruining will be proportional to the intensity of such qualities. People who nurtured demonic qualities to a greater degree will reach the demonic realms and will be remembered as the enemies of the human race for generations to come.

Misconceptions on Restraining Senses: A major misconception that is floated by those who promote demonic habits is that "the best way to tame sensual pleasures is to taste them in an unhindered manner till you develop an aversion for them". Remember that, involving in sensual pleasures is like adding fuel to a fire. More we dwell in them, the more they rage, and the more powerful they become. The heat of such flame becomes unmanageable. It can burn the very integrity of the individual.

Unhindered sensual pleasures make the person like a light worm which gets attracted by the glowing lamp, spends its full time revolving around it and finally perishes by falling into the fire (Gita XI:29). Enjoying unrestrained sensual pleasures is never a solution to come out of the bondage to senses.

Another misconception is that Gita or other Hindu scriptures promote relinquishing sensual pleasures completely. It is not true. Bhagavad Gita is not against desires as long as they are pursued through Dharmic means (Gita VII:11).

The next major misconception is 'one must renounce professional and family life and leave the materialistic world to work for his or her upliftment'. Gita never promotes inaction (renunciation of action) (Gita XVIII:5). It recommends facing everything in life courageously with a pure heart. It recommends acting without fear or favour (Gita V:3). It recommends that we should not cling to results. Learn the art of moving ahead and focusing on the task at hand without getting distracted by the success or failures of previous actions. Face every obstacle in life as if you have already won it. Take up the task as if it is only a formality to register your victory over it (Gita XI:33).

True Struggle in Sensual Control: Restraining senses means not merely physically controlling them yet mentally dwelling on them (Gita III:6). Such people who mentally dwell in the thoughts of sensual pleasures are hypocrites and plaster saints (Vimudha as per Gita III:6). Mental detachment from sensual pleasures is the true meaning of restraining senses (Gita III:7). At will, if person can trigger a state of indifference towards sensual pleasures, then it indicates that, the person has won over the senses and his mind is matured to face bigger battle of life (Gita II:52,53). It comes with dispassion stemming from true knowledge (Patanjali Yoga Sutras Chapter I.15).

The biggest riddle in the spiritual journey is the confusion over the question of *"unless one acquires the knowledge, he cannot tame senses and unless one tames the senses, one cannot acquire knowledge. Which among these two should precede ?".* Breaking this complex interlock is a true challenge to any seeker. To break this riddle, one needs to put in a systematic effort. Great seers like Patanjali in his Yoga Sutras and Almighty himself in Bhagavad Gita have recommended methods to break this riddle. The simple answer to this riddle is, to focus on purifying the mind and attaining control of the senses while having the company of evolved soul (physically or through meditation or their teachings). This will ensure that the riddle is resolved (Gita IV:34).

Till Divinity is tasted by mind, it cannot become still. On the other hand, Divinity cannot be tasted without having a calm mind. The best way to overcome this riddle is to seek Satsanga (the company of Noble Souls)

In presence of noble souls wisdom dawns on the individuals. As wisdom dawns on the mind of an individual, it starts charring the perverted qualities and results of previous perverted actions (Gita IV: 37). Thus, steady progress in the path of self-realization will be ensured in the company of noble people. For those who cannot afford to find the right association, the best way to have it is Svadhyaya (Reading and comprehending the texts having noble thoughts) as described in Patanjali Yoga Sutra Chapter II.1.

Those who have the fortune of having the association with wise and learned souls can engage with them. For the sake of seekers, Bhagavad Gita has listed a few qualities of God realized souls, so that seekers do not fall prey to plaster saints.

How to Identify a God-Realized Person: Look for the following qualities to identify whether the person has the wisdom derived from Divinity, whether he can light up path to divinity.

• Affectionate and compassionate towards all and promotes the well-being of every living being (Gita XII:13)

• Takes the criticism & praise equally. Dwells in Self, untouched by the previous actions (Gita XIV:23-25).

• Steadfast in pursuing the truth, surrenders every moment of life to Almighty (Gita IX:14)

• Able to visualize the presence of Almighty in all beings, and possesses the ability to behold almighty everywhere. Have no longing for physical assets (Gita VI:29,30)

• Treats the rich, poor, pious, sinner, friends, foes and even those who spread hatred with equal compassion and ready to kindle the light of wisdom in all (Gita VI: 9, V:18, Gita XIV: 25).

• Though present actively in the world, can withdraw from distractions like a tortoise withdrawing its limbs at will (Gita II:52). On the other hand, always awake, alert and making incessant efforts to evolve to behold the super soul (Gita II:69).

• Heart is full of the joy of divinity, intellect blossomed with Divine wisdom, lost his temperament in Divine intoxication, senses conquered, greed charred to such an extent that, a piece of gold or a pebble is same (Gita VI:8)

• Sense of peace and tranquillity emanates in his/her presence. Even the animals and birds feel safe in his/her presence renouncing their natural wildness (Patanjali Yoga sutras Chapter II.35).

It is recommended to associate with persons having above qualities. At times it may not be the person who is presently alive, it may be a good book, a sacred location or a person who lived in past. Just hook up with such noble people and their noble thoughts . It will ensure comprehensive victory over the senses.

Once senses are under the control of the mind, now the seeker is ready to take on bigger battles in life to progress and prosper further. He is on the path to attain tranquillity (Gita II:64,65). His mind & intellect are now ready to focus on higher tasks (Gita II:68). On the other hand, a person whose senses have taken over his or her mind, can never be peaceful (Gita II: 66), people who associate with such persons also will feel the disturbances in their journey as the restlessness of such person spill over to others (Gita II:67).

It is difficult to get the right association. However, one can always pray to the Almighty to provide the right association. Pray to Almighty to choose you as his friend, enlighten your intellect, and light up your path. Pray Lord to stand like a lighthouse so that you don't lose sight of the goal of life. Pray to him to give you the power to introspect and correct yourself. When required ask him to act as your king to govern your actions and channel them in the right direction so that you do not get carried away from the right path due to possible distractions by the untamed senses. In your journey to glory, you may feel the waves of heat, and cyclones, but pray to the Almighty to stay with you and see that, you pass safely through the turbulent times. Remember that turbulences in life are short-lived. Those who have the patience to wait will see the peace dawning on the horizon (Gita II:14).

Conclusion: Control over the senses is the prerequisite for success in either the material world or in the spiritual world. To use the mind for the right cause, to firmly stick to the path of knowledge one needs to master the art of detaching from senses at will (Gita II:61). Intellect of such people will blossom whose minds are the masters of their senses. *For those, whose mind has surrendered to their senses, their fall in life is written on the wall.* They are accumulating sin and perpetuating their ignorance. The consequences of sin are elaborated on in the next chapter. Those who are advancing firmly in their quest to tame the senses should seek the right associations. Methods for taming and sharpening the mind and attaching it firmly to the inner intellect are discussed in the next chapters.

Chapter VI

Sin: Causes, Consequences & Remedies

Prelude: Sin is the result of actions that are carried out without the purity of heart. It is also the result of inaction. As long as individuals accomplish any act as part of their duty without hatred or selfishness in executing the act, it does not result in sin. Indulging in sensual pleasures is not a sin if the pleasures are derived through righteous means (Gita VII:11).

There are three levels of sin that a human can commit. They are physical, mental, and spiritual with the seriousness of consequences growing in that order. At a higher level of the spiritual journey, any activity carried out with the feeling of "I am the doer" is a sin. Sin has the quality of hindering progress at the physical, mental and spiritual levels. They bring calamity to the individual's life. The present theme of sin is extracted from various chapters of the Bhagavad Gita.

Sin at Physical Level: At the physical level, not executing the activity that is mandated for the individual is a sin (Gita III:4). Every individual is supposed to execute certain works. For instance, for students, making the best effort to excel in their studies is the mandated action. Similarly, there are duties defined for every individual as a son or daughter, as a father, as a mother, as a friend or relative, as a citizen of the country, as an employee or an employer. Not discharging natural responsibilities is a sin (Gita XVIII:45,46,47).

"One who discharges his duty with pure heart, one who worships Almighty through his work, one who tunes to Divine conscience within while discharging the duties never incurs sin (Gita XVIII:45,46,47)"

Some people search for strong excuses for why they are not discharging their duties (Gita II:4-6). But even the strongest excuse that one can find cannot save them from incurring sin. While not discharging the responsibilities is a sin, running away from responsibilities by looking at the obstacles or challenges is more sinful (Gita II.31,33, III.4).

One must understand that in this world, everyone is always involved in some or other activity (Gita III:5). Even the most unproductive, perverted person is also acting at every moment. Instead of acting in an unorganized manner, it is required to organize the actions so that they will accomplish the intended responsibilities. This will save us from accumulating sin.

Those who earn their living and resources through wrong, unethical or immoral means are sinning (Gita XVI.12). Those who earn their resources only to fulfil their greed and lust without any intention of using them for right means are sinning (Gita XVI.13).

Those who do not thank the Almighty for the physical resources got and use them for their selfish desires accumulate sin (Gita III:13).

Consequences of Sins at Physical Level: Deceleration of personal progress, and loss of reputation in society are some of the consequences (Gita III:35,36).

Sin at Mental Level: If someone thinks by renouncing all physical actions, he or she is going to get rid of any more sin, then it is his ignorance. One has to understand that mind always keeps working by dwelling on various thoughts one after another. This is also an activity. The kind of thoughts the mind nurtures can also make the individual sinner or a sacred individual.

Some of the thoughts that make an individual to accumulate sin are as follows.

(i) Someone who strongly restrains his senses mentally, yet always dwells in the thoughts of sensual pleasures is a sinner (Gita III:6). Hindu Scriptures / Gita never promotes anyone to stop enjoying sensual pleasures completely. It only says, to follow the "righteousness (Dharma) while deriving happiness from senses". When sensual pleasures are derived through the right means, it will not make the concerned a sinner (Gita VII:11). Desires are the driving force for growth. *Desires, which are not against "righteousness" will not bring sin but rather add to the prosperity of individuals as well as to the community.* When the mind promotes senses to satisfy the desires by wrong means, then it brings sin thus ruining the self as well as the society where such individuals live.

(ii) Even after meeting necessities, if anyone stretches himself beyond his physical capacity it is a sin at the mental level because it is the desire in the mind that is forcing the body to stretch further (Gita III:8).

(iii) Carrying out any action with the intent of lust, hatred or intent borne out of arrogance, revenge is sinful (Gita III:37).

(iv) Thinking that I am the doer, and not able to recognise the Divine force present within the body, which is driving the action is a sin (Gita III:27, XVIII:61).

(v) Carrying a feeling of nobility based on the birth is a sin (Gita XVI:15). Inability to treat and give due respect to all other beings, is indirectly insulting the almighty who is equally present in all other beings. Such a person is committing a great sin at the mental level (Gita XVI:19).

Consequences of Sin at the Mental Level: It is more dangerous than sin at the physical level. It acts like a wildfire burning the reserves of the accumulated merit of previous good deeds thus engulfing the individual from all sides, charring his reputation, and social standing there by making his life miserable in this world as well as the worlds he may reach after his death (Gita III:8). It destroys the previously gained knowledge and obscures the wisdom of the individual (Gita III:41). It can attract bad friendship/association which in turn acts as a catalyst for more ruining. People who preached and practised violent thoughts leading to injury and loss of life of fellow beings, people who lived a life of arrogance & unbound selfishness, and people who flexed their muscles against the weak are committing sin which will make them fall into hell (Gita XVI: 13-16).

Sin at Spiritual Level: Identifying the individuals as mere products of the union of male and female without accepting the concept of reincarnation of souls is a sin (Gita XIII: 8). Inability to accept that the almighty is omnipresent is a sin (Gita XVI:8). Denouncing the incarnations of the Lord as mere human beings is a sin (Gita IX:11).

• The inability to identify the all-pervading and omnipotent, omnipresent God and the inability to accept that, all forms of satvik prayers (Prayers done with pure heart irrespective of religious practice) reach the same supreme soul is a spiritual ignorance which can bring sin at spiritual level (Gita VII: 21,22).

• Practicing religious austerities for merely personal gains, practicing religion to show that they are superior or knowledgeful, preaching something only to show their knowledge to others are various forms of spiritual sin (Gita IX:12).

• Invoking the spiritual forces through evil practices is a sin (Gita IX: 12, XVII:4). Those who carry out their penances by troubling their bodies, and those who trouble their senses in the name of the practice of austerities are sinning. Such practices are against the practices recommended by the scriptures (Gita XVII: 5,6).

Consequences of Sins at the Spiritual Level: It is to be understood that, Sin means ignorance. Accumulating sins means accumulating ignorance. The result of spiritual ignorance is restlessness in this world and after death. Such people cannot overcome the cycle of repeated births and deaths (Gita IX:3).

People who preferred evil religious practices will be banished to such worlds where evil forces live (Gita IX: 25). They may take many births in demonic realms before regaining the discretion of a normal human and thus get eligibility to take birth again as a human being. This is the result of promoting and practising the demonic qualities (Gita XVI: 19,20). People who practiced violence in the name of religion, who injure or persecute the weak will reach hell where life is not a celebration but rather a struggle (Gita XVI:13-16).

Special Case of Sin and Method to Cleanse it: Those who carry out the actions with a feeling that 'I am the doer', and don't recognise the Divine driving force behind the action, accumulate a different grade of sin, which acts as a rope drawing the individual again and again into the earthly world (Gia II:51). Results accumulated out of such actions may bring happiness in this life and may bestow them with the ability to reach heaven after death provided their actions are intended for a good cause and executed in the right manner (Gita IX:21, Gita VI:41). But the ignorance that they nurtured that 'I am the doer' and their selfish expectations, will act as a rope to draw them back to the earthly planet from heaven once their reserves of fruits of good deeds were paid off with the reward of a comfortable stay at the heaven (GitaVI:40,41). They need to restart their journey afresh. This cycle will get repeated till the individual overcomes the feeling of 'I am the doer'. This cycle will continue till one nurture the wisdom of offering the 'will to act as well as the results of the action to the almighty'. Those who break this last thread of sin can fix their mind on the Almighty with uninterrupted devotion. This is the state of Nirvana (Liberation of the soul). To break this last thread of sin one needs to practice the austerities prescribed in the scriptures which will be described in subsequent chapters.

How to Cleanse Sin: Surrender the ego

.

"Surrender the ego. Be one with the Almighty. Even a very wicked person can get cleansed of all sins with such one-pointed devotion towards Almighty (Gita IX: 29,30,31) & (Gita XVIII:66)"

Conclusion: Bhagavad Gita, other sacred Indian scriptures and practices can expand the identity of the individual from the body to the soul (Gita XVIII:61), then further expand the identity of the soul within to the soul present in all beings (Gita VI:29). It can cleanse all sins and free the individuals from the consequences of all past actions. Even a small step (Svalpamapi) taken in the direction of Divine wisdom, as prescribed in the scriptures, can save the individual from great perils (Gita II: 40).

To expand the intellect of the individual to behold such a higher state, one must understand the levels of consciousness of individuals, and the result of actions done by individuals under the siege of various levels of consciousness. It is elaborated on in the next chapter.

Chapter VII

Levels of Consciousness, Causes of Misery and Methods to Mitigate

Prelude: Having understood what brings ignorance and imposes sin on individual, one has to understand that we are not the mere body rather we are the consciousness attached to this body. Everyone is a bundle of consciousness which keeps swinging between various levels. One should know what these levels of consciousness are. This is essential to master the art of elevating the consciousness to a level where neither the day-to-day disturbances and disappointments in life can depress, nor the joy of day-to-day successes can hinder further evolution (Gita II:56). Almighty himself revealed the tips on tuning with the eternal (Gita II:39-41). This chapter brings out the essence of what Lord Krishna has told on having Divine consciousness.

"One need not sit and meditate to behold the consciousness of Paramatma. One need to nurture the consciousness of Almighty in every act be it art, music, or day to day responsibilities. Those whose consciousness is steadfastly focused on Almighty, whose intellect & self is absorbed in Almighty get cleansed of all past sins (Gita V:17)".

The Hierarchy of Self Consciousness: Every individual is conscious of himself or herself. But the question is how they are identifying themselves. Is he identifying as merely a body and mind combination or something beyond that (Gita III:42). To elevate the self beyond the realms of body consciousness, one should understand levels of consciousness in which our consciousness can dwell (Gita 2.41).

The primary level of consciousness: Five sensory organs, the mind constitutes this level. People who are conscious of only these objects believe they are merely a combination of body & mind (Gita: III:27). They neither see inward to go beyond the mind to listen to their inner soul nor understand the concept of law or Karma (Gita III:29). In this group, there are two subgroups. The first subgroup constitutes those whose sensory organs control their mind. They are Tamasik or in short retrograde. People who dwell more in this level of consciousness will become enemies to themselves and humanity. They sin out of a passion for sensory pleasures or for satisfying their retrograde beliefs. The words of wise men or scriptures will go in vain when told to such people (Gita

III:29). Till they suffer heavily because of their own mistakes, the realization will not descend into their minds.

For the other subgroup in this category, the mind is not under the control of the senses, but it spends its time and energy to realize personal gains. The success of such people is short-lived. Since the mind is fixed on personal gains and egoistic feelings, they are bound to get influenced by the failures and successes in life. Their journey goes on without a fixed pattern or philosophy. Their progress in life is cyclic because meagre and momentary personal gains made by stepping out of Dharma vanish when the Law of Karma catches them and pulls them back to square one. Thus, effectively their progress becomes nil (Gita XVI: 12,16).

Such people lose their composure in both failures and successes. Depression during failure breaks their heart and success corrupts their mind. Sometimes they become overconfident, yet other times, they lose their self-confidence.

Their successes are short-lived. They are ignorant, confused, unfocussed, fickle minded and doubtful of everything. They neither achieve anything worthy in their life nor allow others to progress. They ruin themselves and the institutions that they are attached to (Gita IX:11, IV:40).

Second Level of Consciousness (Gita III: 42, 43): Intellect and Wisdom are the second levels of consciousness. Intellect is the sum of what one has learned and understood in life, on the other hand, Wisdom is divine and flows down from the heavens as and when sought by the intellect. Whenever intellect turns inward for guidance from within, it ignites the spark of wisdom. As wisdom emanates from the soul within, it carries noble thoughts filled with righteousness, compassion, courage, self-control etc. Those who dwell more in this state of consciousness where intellect derives its strength from the wisdom within, prosper in life. The more the intellect tunes in with wisdom, the more they progress. Irrespective of the position they attain in life, they become a role model to the people around them (Gita III:21).

Ideally, at this level of consciousness, the mind should listen to intellect, and intellect in turn listen to wisdom emanating from the Soul within. However, the mind tries to take control of the intellect. The intellect of untrained individuals sometimes acts as a master to the mind and sometimes as its servant.

Thus, the human intellect is always in a state of confusion on, whether to follow the path of wisdom or the path preferred by the mind and senses (Gita III: 39). Even the most learned feel the raging struggle within till they firmly behold the third level of consciousness.

Thus, the second level of consciousness is the key for deciding which direction the person is moving, whether advancing towards eternal blissful consciousness that is in store at the third level, or back to the first level where the pain of failures and pleasures of successes keep perturbing the pleasantness of individual self. Most individuals get stuck up at the second level of consciousness. They are confused about how to elevate themselves further as the veil of illusion is so strongly obscuring the wisdom from the intellect (GitaIX:14). One needs sustained efforts to cross this barrier. It is possible with the guidance of a learned individual who crossed this barrier or guidance from scriptures which promote universal consciousness and brotherhood (Gita IV:34).

Third Level of Consciousness: Being conscious of Paramatma within, and the ability to see the same Paramatma in all beings is the culmination of this level of consciousness (Gita VI:29). Tuning with the consciousness of all-pervading divine, the ability to behold the almighty everywhere and ability visualize everything within Almighty, ability to see through his (almighty) eyes, think through his heart, execute actions as per his will is the ultimate stage in this level of consciousness (Gita VI:30). Those who attain this stage will not have anything different from Almighty himself and thus find equanimity with the Almighty (Gita VI:32). They are elevated to a level which is beyond the cycle of life and death. This is called Kaivalya or Salvation. This is the goal of every individual. Knowingly or unknowingly every individual is progressing towards it. Some learn the hard lessons before turning to this path whereas others tune themselves with the learned souls to take a flight to this level (Gita IV:34).

The cause of misery: The question which every seeker of divinity puts forth is, "O lord, please let me know, impelled by what force does a person commit sin against his wish and drive himself/herself into miseries? What is that force, that tempts us to sin against our conscience

175

and forces us into frustration and misery (GitaIII:36)". Lord says that the six enemies namely **anger, lust, greediness, false attachment, pride, and jealousy pull us into the world of misery.** The most dangerous among them are anger and lust. The more indulgence in them more they rage thereby making the individual sinful (Gita III:37).

These endemic qualities do not let the mind dwell on the Divine within us and thus pervert the intellect. One with a perverted intellect becomes his enemy and executes the tasks to his ruin and imposes misery on himself or herself. It is very difficult to come out of the clutches of these endemic forces without a cautious effort. Thus, misery is the result of thoughts and actions carried out while dwelling too much in the first level of consciousness where the above-mentioned six enemies are very strong.

Misery is also a result of one's failure to elevate the self to see the Divine sparkle inside which is ever witnessing our thoughts and deeds. Misery is also the result of failure to repent for past mistakes and sins. It is also the result of our failure to seek asylum at the feet of the Almighty who only yearns for wilful prayer and heartfelt surrender (Gita IX:22).

The Lord says, "Every human being is bestowed with the Divine wisdom and discretion by the Divine mother (Referred to as Prakriti in Sankhya texts)" Divine mother has built our body as a chariot for our journey with, the sensory organs as its horses, mind as its reins to control the horses, the buddhi (intellect) as the discretion to take the intended path our journey (Katha Upanishad). Jeevatma is sitting as the charioteer (Gita III:42).

For the journey to be successful, one must use the wisdom of discrimination borne out of the churning of intellect by the mind. But unfortunately, the six endemic qualities surround the intellect like the smoke engulfs and dims the fire. Their intellect is disconnected from the Divine wisdom and the mind derives nothing useful from it. Under such circumstances, the Jeevatma within (Jeevatma) cannot make any purposeful journey and thus wander endlessly like a lost man in the forest (Gita III: 38,39,40).

"Those who got deluded by the consciousness of the body and sensual pleasure, those who got possessed by ego, lust and anger, those who hate others and thus hate the God present in other bodies can never get relieved from the cycle of repeated births and sufferings (Gita XVI: 18,19). If they don't reform themselves using the opportunities given, they slide

down towards demonic realms after cycle of birth (Gita XVI:20)"

Conclusion: One needs to strengthen the intellect to behold the third level of consciousness. It involves identifying the self as a Soul, not a mere body. From such consciousness, one needs to derive strength for the mind. Spiritual consciousness spreads at three levels. They are the consciousness of the Atman (Soul or Jeevatma), the Consciousness of Divine Mother (Prakriti or Mother Goddess Parvati) and the Consciousness of Paramatma (Almighty or Super soul). When one rises above the body consciousness, he can behold the wisdom pronounced by the Bhagavad Gita regarding the Divine Trinity and their interrelationship. To rise to such a level, one needs to carry out various austerities. These austerities are discussed in subsequent chapters.

Chapter VIII

Righteousness from Religion and Righteousness for the Religion

(Austerities for Body, Mind, Heart, and Intellect)

Prelude: The essence of the Bhagavad Gita lies in its emphasis on the austerities of Dharma (virtues). It recommends shedding the wrong attitudes like arrogance, selfishness, anger, jealousy etc. and recommends cultivating the habit of identifying the spark of the Almighty present in every being (Gita XVI: 18). It recommends the austerities for the body, austerities for speech, austerities for heart, austerities for intellect and the methods to synergize them to bask in peace and tranquillity. This section deals with the practice of austerities that can elevate individuals to behold the tranquillity of the Almighty. One must understand that, though austerities of body, mind, heart and intellect are dealt with separately, in practice they are highly intertwined. They are to be practised together. These austerities of body, mind, heart and intellect are the recommended Righteous (Dharma) practices by religion that are discussed in this chapter. However in addition to it, righteousness for the religion is also discussed. This is included to caution devotees to not to misinterpret the scriptures and go against the basic human values.

Austerities of the Body: Respecting teachers, elders, learned scholars, and celestial beings, practising the brahmacharya (being celibate and walking with God), being nonviolent, and maintaining physical cleanliness of the body and surrounding (Soucha in Sanskrit) are the austerities recommended for the body (Gita XVII:14). As per Patanjali yoga sutras, Practicing the 'Yama" is the first step towards the self-realization. Yama is austerity for the body. It involves being nonviolent, speaking the truth, keeping away from stealthy or secret activities which are against Dharma (asteya), being celibate, and not owning other's property (Aparigraha). Asana (posture) is also an austerity for the body. It involves strengthening the body to sustain long hours of concentrated effort by sitting in one place. This ability stems from the combination of a strengthened body and mind. To attain such a state, one must eat only sufficient food (neither in excess nor less), and should have a controlled sleeping habit (Gita VI:16). One should take food, which is fresh, which can impart strength to the body, easy to digest. This kind of food not only nourishes the body but also promotes a healthy mind (Gita XVII:8). Food which is too sour or bitter or hot or too saline, which is dry, and not easy to digest are to be minimized (Gita XVII:9). Food, which is not fresh, food which releases strong smell and impure food is to be avoided (Gita XVII:10). One must understand that food is the source of life (Gita III:14). It can give vitality to body and mind. One who does not have the right food consciousness can never prosper in any field leave alone the spiritual journey. One who does not earn his or her food through the right means also can never prosper. Food that we eat should be worthy to offer as an offering to God. Such food can give a strong body and peaceful mind (Gita II:65).

Austerities of body and mind includes controlling the senses as well. Elaborate discussions on the Austerities of senses are made in the previous chapters. Partly donating hard-earned money to the needy is also part of austerity. However, donating it to the right person at a suitable time and place is essential to make it as an austerity (Gita XVII:20). One should know that the body is a tool to practice the Dharma. The body is provided to us to use as a tool to elevate the Jeevatma. Even for bare maintenance of the body one has to any way act. No one can sit without action (Gita III:8). Hence best way is to treat every work as an offering to the Almighty. It will elevate the self (IX:27).

Austerities of the Mind: Mind is the storehouse of Samskaras (the integrated treasure of imprints of experiences). Before any experience fades away from the active memory, it leaves its imprint on the mind. As per the Yoga Sutras of Patanjali, there are five states for the mind (Refer to Patanjali Yoga Sutras Chapter I:5 onwards). Mind dwells in either of these five states. They are

• Right Knowledge,

• Error or Misconception,

• Imagination,

• Sleep,

• Memorizing past events.

While the first four states of the mind can be understood and streamlined with some effort, memory is difficult to bring under control. It keeps revisiting even when trying to resist with full force. It is difficult to tame. It needs prolonged practice to control the memory. Bhagavad Gita and Patanjali Yoga Sutras have certain recommendations on how to control the memory of past events.

The mind can be brought under control through the practice of detachment and dispassion towards praises and abuses, success and failures (Gita VI:35). Detachment also includes overcoming the craving for sensual pleasures (Patanjali Yoga Sutras Chapter I: 15).

Once the above state is achieved, the mind develops the ability to get absorbed into a state of Samprangya (a state of consciousness) where it can penetrate the subtleness of the purpose of an object or activity. In this state mind experiences the radiating bliss of being not ignorant of anything seen or unseen (Patanjali Yoga Sutras Chapter I: 17). It starts experiencing the present moment which is not interrupted by unwanted memories. This is the austerity of mind in brief. (For more detailed explanations readers are advised to refer to Yoga Sutras of Patanjali and Commentary on it by Dr Edwin F Bryant, North Point Press).

Austerities of the heart are one step higher than the austerities of the body and mind. As part of the austerities of the heart, one has to cultivate Satvik (nonviolence, compassion, purity, truth) thoughts. One must understand that the Satvik action of the body is the result of Satvik thoughts of mind and heart. To cultivate Satvik thought, one should control the agitation of mind, should be pleasant, and should practice silence towards unnecessary things and should cultivate utmost faith in the Almighty (Gita XVII:16). *Being violent means losing faith in God, it is an indication of fallen minds.*

Satvik thoughts and actions can be nurtured with the practice of the following.

• Karma Yoga or Doing the action while renouncing the fruits of action is the primary requirement to condition the heart (Gita XVII:11). If it is not practised, the memories of missed opportunities, failures and successes will hunt for a long time thereby disturbing individual's peace. Karma Yoga can also enable the individual to live in present. Those who do not practice Karma yoga, will find themselves stuck to the past or clinging to the imagination of the future (Gita II:11). Hence the wise must follow the path of Karma Yoga,

• Reading, reciting, and comprehending sacred texts which promote universal harmony, practising the path that wishes the wellbeing of entire humanity irrespective of their profession, religious denomination (Gita V:25, XVI: 1),

• Not initiating any action just for the sake of getting accolades or appreciation, nor carrying out any activity just for the sake of showing off (Gita XVII:12),

• Not taking up any action half-heartedly, Not eating food that is sourced through unvirtuous means (Gita XVII: 13),

- Attaining a state which is comparable to the ocean, which does not change its boundaries or losses its composure though there is continuous flooding of river water (Gita II:70),

- Ability to be impartial in decision-making by getting rid of previous likes and dislikes and the ability to stay alert in the present (Gita IV: 23, Gita II: 11),

- Carrying the consciousness of the all-pervading Paramatma, carrying out all activities with a feeling in the heart that, the all-pervading Lord is observing all the activities, carrying a feeling that the urge for initiation of the concerned work is triggered by God himself, being fearless, free from selfishness (Gita V: 17),

- Conditioning the heart to take both the praises and criticisms equally. One has to understand it is not being indifferent, it is about not being carried away based on someone's praises or criticism (Gita XII:19)

- Ability to ensure that, the sadness does not become depression and the happiness doesn't elevate to a level where the reality is obscured (Gita II:56).

Wise people make use of the present moment completely. They Do not let the hangover of the past or fascination for the future derail the present (Gita II:11). Know that sorrows or happiness in life come and go like seasons. Train the mind to bear them without getting imbalanced by these temporary cyclic guests (Gita II:14).

If the above qualities are nurtured it elevates the individual's heart towards the Paramatma. The heart triggers the speech and speech reflect the heart. The heart, which is pure, unbiased, peaceful in its outlook,

184

heart which is trained to control the temptations of mind and senses, the heart which enjoys dwelling in silence or the stillness of the thoughts, the heart which keeps refining itself is the heart which is practising the austerities (Gita XVII:16).

Austerities of the Speech: The words spoken by the individual depict the essence of his or her personality. Ancient Indian texts treated speech as the physical manifestation of the spark of conscious energy of Manah (heart) which developed the urge (Sankalpa in Sanskrit) to manifest. The activity of talking also is also a kind of Prayer or austerity. It should be done with humbleness and seriousness. One should be cautious while talking. Speech should be used for the right cause. Shankaracharya in his famous writing by the name 'Sadhana Panchakam' advised seekers not to utter even one word without a positive purpose attached to it.

Such a high degree of wisdom towards the words is not possible unless, the person nurtures integrity, dignity, and Divine wisdom. As long as these qualities are not present in the heart, one can't practice the austerities of words. The 17th Chapter of the Bhagavad Gita gives suggestive discourses on how to purify the heart and speech. As per the Bhagavad Gita, Austerities of speech include *"speaking the words which are not laced with bad emotions, speaking the truth which results in happiness and peace, reciting the sacred texts"*.

Reciting the sacred sound 'Om' before initiating any activity is also part of the austerities of speech (Gita XVII:24). Tuning the words with the heart, speaking what is in the heart and walking the talk is the best austerity.

There should be no difference between what is thought, what is spoken and finally what is implemented. Thus heart, speech and body form the three tools of austerities. Synergizing them maximises the benefits in both the material and spiritual world (Gita XVII:14).

Above austerities can elevate the human consciousness to the higher realms where he or she can behold true wisdom.

Austerities of the Intellect: There is nothing noble than the wisdom borne out of blossomed intellect. One whose intellect is blossomed, can effortlessly behold the ultimate state of spiritual bliss (Gita IV:38). Austerities of intellect involve the practice of seeing the Almighty as all-pervading. Almighty is the wisdom in the wise people. He is the eternal spark of all beings (Gita VII: 10). Recognizing the almighty as the heroism in the heroic deeds and the strength of strong people is part of the austerities of intellect (Gita VII:11). Effort to recognize that the radiance in all glowing objects like moon, sun and the stars, tastelessness of water, taste in the tasteful items, the mystical sound "Om" in Vedas, urge for the spiritual progress in the Yogis, sweet fragrance of the earth, glow in the fire, spark of seed force of life in all beings as the extended manifestation of Almighty is an Austerity of Intellect (Gita VII: 6-10).

In general, intellect is not strong enough to experience the all-pervading Almighty, as the intellect was carried away by the disturbing proportions of the three basic qualities (Sattva, Rajas & Tamas) (Gita VII:13).

To gain blossomed intellect to behold Almighty in every aspect of life, incessant practice of righteous path over many births, rigorous practice of austerities of body, mind and heart are required (Gita VII: 19). Those who successfully establish themselves in the path of austerities of intellect, realizes that it is one supreme Soul that is answering everyone's prayers, it is the one supreme soul that is blessing every one irrespective of their methods of prayer (Gita VII:20).

What is Righteousness (Dharma) for the Religion: In this chapter so far, the emphasis is on, the austerities of body, mind and heart. It was repeatedly emphasized that these austerities are to be guided by Dharma or Righteousness. Many times, conflict arises on what constitutes Dharma or Righteousness. In every religion, there exists a conflict between those who want moderation of the customs and those who want to impose the customs rigidly. There exists conflicting interpretations or misinterpretations of the scriptures over which different groups argue on what is right or wrong. This section is added to deal with such a dilemma.

Bhagavad Gita recommends taking guidance from the standard religious scriptures to decide on what is to be done or what not to be done (Gita XVI:24). Bhagavad Gita, Upanishads, Yoga Sutras of Patanjali and Vedas are the treasures which can be referred as standard texts on dos and don'ts. These texts have identified what is right and what is wrong. A summary of the same is given below.

One has to understand that, any practice which is against human values can never be the right path for spiritual progress. Human values like respecting individual dignity and liberty, being compassionate towards all, wishing for the welfare of all irrespective of their denomination, and treating everyone with the same respect and love can never be compromised in the name of religious practice (Gita XII:13). If anyone is acting against such values, it will only take him or her towards the destruction. One has to understand that the Almighty is one and he loves everyone equally. By hating anyone based on their birth, religion etc. the individual is hating the Almighty himself. This is because, Almighty is present in everybody (Gita XVI:18). Any religious practice done with hatred brings more wickedness.

Practising the Dharma of love is unconditional. It should encompass both friends and foes, those who criticize you or praise you or those who follow the path that you follow and those who do not follow (Gita XII:18,19). One who practices such a high level of Dharma will soon feel the sweetness of the Divine nectar. Almighty will shower his blessings on such an individual (Gita XII:20).

If any religious practice conflicts with the dignity of human beings, if any practice is instigating violence, if any practice is disturbing harmony, then it can never be a real religious practice. Probably it could be due to misinterpretation of religious texts such practices could have crept in and got established as a custom. So, any such custom if found, should be discarded to maintain the pristine purity of the religion.

If someone proclaims that the path that he is practising is the only right path, if someone could not tolerate logical questioning, could not allow expansion of knowledge and thus confines the human mind in a narrow boundary, then he is working against humanity. He is making religion against the natural inquisitive nature of the human mind and thus working against the creativity bestowed on us by God (Gita XVIII:22).

One must understand that the religious thoughts propounded by the seers are like flowing Ganges which were brought down from the heavens for the sake of upliftment of many souls. If one takes the plunge in it with utmost faith and with surrendered ego it will cleanse all sins. On the other hand, if one practices the religion with ego, hatred, selfishness, narrow mindedness, then he or she is polluting the religion. One must understand that practices like religious rituals, attire we assume, costumes we wear, and the language we speak can change and should be allowed to change with time. It is essential to accommodate changing lifestyles, changing professions, changing places of work and the type of work. It is not against the Dharma. But what should never change is the respect for basic human values, the accommodative spirit of religion, the ability to recognize and celebrate the unbound potential of humans to evolve themselves into liberated souls, having respect for the Law of Karma, utmost faith in the eternal all-pervading Almighty. These are the boundaries of righteousness for the religion.

Conclusion: One who firmly follows the path of Dharma (righteousness), who strengthens the body through a disciplined life, practices dispassion towards sensual pleasures, sheds the qualities of arrogance, jealousy, narrow mindedness, one who cultivates the quality of compassion towards all, practices to see the Almighty in every being, one who trains the mind to penetrate the subtle purpose of every act can get an accelerated elevation towards the blissful state of self-realization. Reforming one's own body, mind and heart is the essential first step to succeed in the path of spirituality. It may take a prolonged time to train and condition the body, mind, and heart to act as tools to elevate the soul (Patanjali Yoga Sutras Chapter I:14). However, more intense is the practice of the austerities recommended for body, mind, and heart more accelerated will be the spiritual progress (Patanjali Yoga Sutras Chapter I: 21)

Chapter IX

Trinity of Basic Qualities: The Real Driving Force

Prelude: Three primitive qualities namely Satvik (Purity, Knowledge and Harmony), Rajasik (Passion and Vigour), and Tamasik (Inaction, Laziness and Ignorance) are the primary qualities that emerge when Jeevatma starts interacting with twenty-four facets of Prakriti. These qualities bind the Jeevatma with the body and dwarf its vision (Gita XIV: 5-7). These three qualities can also be counted as three primitive energies of nature. Thus, Prakriti throws a veil of delusion which is made up of three primitive qualities. The liberation involves breaking this veil and thus freeing the Jeevatma from bondage (Gita XIV: 19,20). This section deals with the description of the veil of delusion and the methods to break the veil.

"When one develops the intellect to perceive that his actions are being driven by three basic qualities of Satvika, Rajasika and Tamasik and understands that the veil of delusion made of these three qualities is thrown around his intellect, then his real self-start perceiving the Divine wisdom. Such a person can behold the Almighty who is above three basic qualities. He attains liberation from sorrows, diseases and ultimately from the cycle of birth and death (Gita XIV:19,20)"

The Nest of Delusion: Everyone gets into the charm of three basic qualities which obscure the vision. Karmic remnants of the individual and his or her past association with the three qualities decide how much of each quality he or she will tap into this life. This becomes their starting balance which decides their temperament, and inclinations in this life. One who steadfastly practices the path of righteousness and offers the fruits of action to the Maheswara (Almighty) gets cleansed of all previous Karmic remnants and reaches the shores of Divine wisdom (Gita XVI:5). To practice the path of righteousness one should develop the discrimination to differentiate between the three basic qualities. One should understand that though the veil of delusion is made up of Satvika, Rajasika and Tamasik guans, the quality of Satva has Divinity inbuilt into it. It can free the self from delusion whereas the other two qualities bind the self to the cycle of repeated births (Gita XVI:5).

One should understand that three basic qualities pervade everything in this world. They encompass every act of the universe. They permeate the Knowledge, the knower, and the Knowing. They permeate the Action, Doer, and Purpose of the act (Gita XVIII:18,19). How each of the three basic qualities namely Satvik, Rajasik and Tamasik gives different results is elaborated in this section.

Knowledge from the Perspective of Three Basic Qualities: Satvik outlook enables the individual to see the Almighty as the common and single indestructible entity present in all beings yet manifesting in diverse forms (Gita XVIII:20). Rajasik outlook sees the Almighty as a separate entity from his creation and beings. Thus, it disables the individual's vision to see the Almighty present in all being (Gita XVIII:21). Tamasik outlook promotes logicless thoughts. It promotes narrow-mindedness. It never allows the individual to ponder deeply on the knowledge enriching thoughts (Gita XVIII:22).

Types of Actions from the Perspective of Three Basic Qualities: Action which is triggered by the wisdom gained from the scriptures and self-control with the vast knowledge of the pros and cons of the work well evaluated before its initiation is a Satvik act. It is not initiated or executed for mere self-satisfaction. It is neither influenced by personal likes and dislikes, nor executed for personal gains (Gita XVIII:23). Actions which are not backed by the wisdom and deep understanding of the method of execution, yet initiated to satisfy one's ego, carried out in hurry thus exhausting the individual during the execution of the tasks is called Rajasik act (Gita XVIII:24). Tasks which are done without bothering for consequences of violence, loss of life, which is initiated without assessing one's strength, resources and capacity are Tamasik acts. They are generally initiated due to emotional imbalance, and false fascination (Gita XVIII:25).

Types of Doers (One who Executes Action) from the Perspective of Three Basic Qualities: One who is free from sensual temptations, not boasting as the 'I am' the doer, who is courageous and enthusiastic, who is not imbalanced by the momentary failures or meagre successes is the Satvik Doer (Gita XVIII: 26). One who wishes to own the gains completely to himself, who gets agitated or even becomes violent by momentary failures, who don't share anything with others (poor team worker) is the Rajasik Doer (Gita XVIII:27). One who does not have self-confidence, who don't have organized day to day life, who cheats others, who disturbs and discourages others, who always moans for trivial losses than focusing on what he could do further, one who takes a too long time or mismanages the time to execute the tasks are the Tamasik Doers (Gita XVIII:28).

Types of Intellect from the Perspective of Three Basic Qualities: Satvik intellect is the one which can differentiate and deploy the knowledge required for a blissful life in the physical and spiritual facets of life. It can trigger activity when required and fold back to hold back from overdoing it. Satvik intellect can keep the individuals away from self-damaging acts yet can give courage when required to stand against the odds (Gita XVIII:30). Rajasik intellect is the one which cannot draw a proper demarcation of the above aspects like physical and spiritual life, action and over action. It confuses the mind and hence blurs decision-making (Gita XVIII:31). Tamasik intellect is the one which makes the individual strongly believe as 'wrong is right'. It does not allow debate as it concludes what is right and what is wrong without proper analysis. It makes illogical and foolish conclusions from everything that is seen (Gita XVIII:32).

Courage and Decisiveness from the Perspective of Three Basic Qualities: Satvik decisiveness involves channelizing all the life forces of senses, mind, and intellect for a noble cause. Satvik decisiveness enables the individual from not getting tempted and diverted from the goal (Gita XVIII:33). Rajasik decisiveness and courage emanate from the strong enthusiasm and willpower to complete the task to gain monetary or sensory pleasures (Gita XVIII:34). Tamasik decisiveness encourages to not to leave laziness, long periods of sleep during the daytime (working times) and not to leave negative thoughts. Tamasik person finds all excuses and strong reasons to live such a life (Gita XVIII:35).

Comfort from the Perspective of Three Basic Qualities: Satvik comfort is the one which is bitter in the beginning yet it transforms slowly into the sweat and comfortable victories in life (Gita XVIII:37). One which gives sensory pleasures in the beginning yet slowly transforms into the bitter experience is the Rajasik comfort (Gita XVIII:38). One which pushes into the delusion of sweet comfort from the beginning to end yet ruining the individual (like laziness, drugs) is the Tamasik comfort (XVIII:39).

The veil made up of the above three basic qualities is three-layered. One who gets filtered into the Tamasik realms will have more suffering. One who reaches the Satvik plane of the nest will experience comfort.

This veil spreads not only on the earth but even for those who live on the Divine planets (XVIII:40).

One who surrenders to the almighty can come out of the spell of the veil (Gita XVIII:66). However, heartful surrender at the feet of the Almighty can happen only when one maximizes the quality of Satvik nature. To maximize the Satvik nature, one must develop a Divine out-ward look towards the creation of God and Divine inward introspection towards his existence.

Subdivisions Under Each of the Qualities: Under the broad division of Satvik quality, there could be further subdivisions. They are Satvika Satvik, Rajasika Satvik and Tamasika Satvik. For instance, practising the spiritual life, donation, and austerities are Satvik acts which have the power to maximize Satvik nature further (Gita XVIII:5). However, each of these Satvik acts can have three different degrees of Satvik thoughts. For instance, donation (Satvika) of the right items donated at right time to the needy and deserving without expecting any favours back (Gita XVII:20) is the Satvika Satvik act. It can dissolve the veil of delusion (maya) as the Tamasik and Rajasik threads of delusion disappear com-pletely. The donation which is done with an expectation of some favour in return or donation not done with a wholehearted feeling of donating is the Rajasik Satvika act (Gita XVII:21). Donating items which were sourced through the wrong means, donating the items with an attitude of throwing, donating at the wrong place, wrong time or to a person who does not deserve to receive is Tamasik donation or Tamasik Satvik (Gita XVII:22). Rajasik and Tamasik donations (good work done with wrong intentions) may not purify the donor though minor transfor-mation in quality towards Satvik nature may get triggered by it.

Similarly, spiritual practices are generally categorized under the Satvik acts. However, if the spiritual practice transforms our attitude to respect the elders, and teachers, gives pure heart, gives broad-mindedness to accommodate every noble thought, and promotes detachment from the results of action then it is a Satvik practice (Gita XVII:15,16,17). Spiritual acts intended to show off are Rajasik acts of spirituality. On the other hand, in the name of spiritual practice if one troubles his own body or aims at the destruction of others is a Tamasik austerity (Gita XVII:18,19).

End Results of Nurturing Three Qualities: No one can sit without action even for a second. Everyone is involved in some or other work (Gita III:5). These actions are driven by the decisions of the mind, in turn, the mind is influenced by the three qualities that it has nurtured. If the Satva is nurtured it suppresses the Rajasik, and Tamasik nature and bestows wisdom and comfort from the acts done (Gita XIV:10,9). If Rajasik thoughts are nurtured, it suppresses the Satvik, and Tamasik qualities and promotes action for sensual pleasures, personal gains, and greediness. Thus, it promotes more and more attachment with the body leading to restlessness (Gita XIV: 8,10,12). When Tamasik nature is nurtured, it suppresses Satvik and Rajasik nature and bestows foolishness, laziness, and inability to utilise the opportunities in life and thus pushes life into peril (Gita XIV:8,10,13).

Result of Three Basic Qualities on Life after Death: Those who nurture the Satvik nature can feel its radiance over time, as the bright light of Satva emanates from all parts of the body (Gita XIV:11). Those who leave their body after attaining such a state will move to higher planets

197

where the diseases, hunger, old age, and other limitations encountered in this planet can't trouble any more (Gita XIV:11,14). They do not come back to earth, as they oriented themselves towards the qualities of wisdom and light (Gita VIII:24). Such a Yogi will move up the ladder of evolution. One who leaves this body after practising the Rajasik nature in this birth, will come back to the earthly planet and take birth among the people who incline to take up activities for personal gains (Gita XIV:12). One who leaves this body after practising the Tamasik nature will take birth among the uncivilized people. If the Tamasik nature is too strongly nurtured, he or she may slide down the ladder of evolution and may take birth as wild animals or birds which fit their temperament (Gita XIV:15). These three qualities form a layer around the soul. At the time of leaving the body the essence of these qualities nurtured by the individual travels along the Soul (Gita XV:8). Prakriti segregates the individual souls based on the qualities that are travelling along with them (Gita IV:13). A few souls which deserve an upward ascent may never come back to the earthly planet. They move upward towards the realms of happiness and bliss. Those who nurtured predominantly Satvik qualities yet not sufficient for permanent promotion to higher realms will stay for a long period in the blissful realms and then descend back to earth. They may be reborn in a family which is wealthier and well-mannered (Gita VI:41). A selected few may get a chance to take birth in a family of Yogis. Getting such birth is a rare gift given to a selected few based on the merit of Satvik qualities they nurtured in previous births (Gita VI:42). Effortlessly they revive the previous practice of maximising the Satvik qualities,

198

and quickly intensify it. By washing off the remanent ego, they cross the final barriers (Gita VI:43,44). Then they ascend to the realms of ultimate bliss (Gita VI:45).

Those who wish to maximise Satvik nature yet are unable to come out from the grip of Rajasik and Tamasik qualities need not feel left behind. They were recommended to choose the profession that fits their temperament. They should do their duty as a service to God. Offer the fruits of action to God. This approach is recommended as the preferred approach. Over time it can calm the mind and enable the Divine intellect to flow in (Gita XII:11,12). One earnest request made to Almighty to save from ignorance is enough to get his immediate assistance (Gita XVIII:66, IX:31).

However, as long as the individual wants to sail on his own Almighty will not interfere. The individual will be solely responsible for his or her upward or downward movement (Gita VI:5, Gita V:15). Mother Goddess Prakriti will deliver what he deserves without any bias. To her all are equal irrespective of whether we are worshipping her or not (Gita IX:29). However, the moment the individuals seek refuge at Almighty (Paramatma), they will find an accelerated ascent towards the Dharmic wisdom, and the bliss born out of it (Gita IX:30,31). God is only a call away. It is a promise given by Paramatma himself that, those who will seek refuge at his feet will never get defeated again. Paramatma told that this statement made by him can be proclaimed loudly to all (Gita IX:31).

Conclusion: The body and mind are the tools for the soul to travel towards ultimate bliss. One needs to involve in the satvik acts and nurture Satvik qualities. Satvik nature can comfort the individual and the people around him. Satvik quality will act as a medium to uplift the soul towards the higher realms where the limitations experienced on the earthly planet like disease, hunger, old age etc—will cease. If the Tamasik qualities are nurtured it will hurt the individual in both physical and spiritual worlds. The spiritual practice aims to transform the individual into a good human being, then to transform the human into Divine. The nest of delusion is made up of three basic qualities. One needs to break this veil to liberate the self.

Chapter X

Concluding Remarks

It is difficult to summarise the message of the Bhagavad Gita and Yoga Sutras in a few words. The summary may miss out on important aspects and approaches for self-realisation. To seek the Divine advice on what to write in conclusive remarks, I spent three days at Holy Vrindavan seeking guidance from the Almighty. A few points that Lord Krishna triggered in my mind during my stay at Vrindavan are given below as a summary.

• Never renounce the Yagya (the act of worshipping the almighty). Carry out every activity of life with a feeling that, it is part of Yagya or worship to God. The results of the action are to be renounced (Gita XVIII:5,6; III: 9,12,13). Though the focus should not be on the results of the actions, the results that trickle down because of dharmic actions should be accepted as a blessing of the almighty (Gita III:9,12,13).

• The sacred act of donation (Dana) to the needy and deserving should never the renounced. (Gita XVIII:5, XVII:20).

• The act of Tapa (austerity) which includes the austerity of body, mind & heart, the austerity of speech, and the austerity of intellect should be practised without fail.

• Action (Karma) or Responsibility should never be renounced. It should be executed at any cost within the constraints of Dharma.

The above four acts namely Yagya (worshipping God), Dana (donation), Tapaha (austerity), and Karma (working to accomplish responsibilities) should never be relinquished. They can purify the individual (Gita XVIII:5).

• Live a life such that no one feels troubled by you. It includes not only human beings but the rest of the living and non-living entities of the world. At the same time, never allow yourselves to get troubled by others. Deal with everyone and every moment without losing the temperament and without bias (Gita XII:15). Under any circumstances, never hate anyone. Be friendly and compassionate towards all (Gita XII:13). Such a person is dearest to the Almighty.

• Do not allow Tamasik nature to take over you. It will drive you towards arrogance, violence, and destruction (Gita XVIII:25). Body is the tool to elevate the Jeevatma. Use it for Satvik acts.

• Jeevatma is all pervasive in the body (Gita XIII:33). Paramatma is present as an observer in everyone (Gita XIII:23). He is the seed present in Jeevatma (Gita VII:10). Paramatma is present both inside and outside of the body. Paramatma is the source of light for the entire universe. For him there is neither near nor far, he is both static and moving (Gita XIII:16). He is above all dualities & never touched by the limitations of time. Rest all in this creation including the Prakriti and Jeevatma shine due to Paramatma (Gita XIII:18,33, 34). The three basic qualities namely Satvik, Rajasik and Tamasik are offshoots of Prakriti. Due to association with Prakriti, these qualities are induced in Jeevatma thereby constraining its true potential. On other hand, Parama Purusha (Paramatma) is never constrained by Prakriti or the qualities of Prakriti (Gita XIII:32).

• Devas (Gods) are celestial beings who have more satvik nature than Humans. Asuras (demons) and animals have more Tamasik nature. The elevation of humans towards Divine realms or demotion towards demonic realms is based on the qualities he or she nurtures in life (Gita XVI). The law of Karma works without any bias. One can cleanse the past sins through repentance, Tapas or surrender to the Almighty.

• The first step in beholding divinity is to become a good human being. One must turn into a good human being by nurturing Satvik thoughts. Once the mind & body are conditioned through Satvik practices, they can act as the right tool to behold divinity. No spiritual practice can elevate human beings as long as Tamasik, and Rajasik qualities are not tamed.

• One must understand that he or she is his/her friend or foe. Almighty never compels anyone for any activity nor wants anyone to merely become a slave in his grand play. Almighty never transgresses into individual's liberty in thoughts and actions, but the results of the same need to be borne by the individual as the Law of Karma will execute itself without any flaw. Almighty will interfere only when his intervention is sought. He has the power to write off the Karmic debt and bless us with intellect to behold him. He is so compassionate that, he can bestow us everything that he holds and make us on par with him.

All-pervading Paramatma is only a call away. He is the only companion through our journey which spanned innumerable births. He is eagerly waiting for our heartfelt request to uplift us.

He is ready to lift us from this chain of repeated births and deaths. Are we ready ?

Chapter XI

Thirty-Two Selected Slokas from Bhagavad Gita

Every Sloka of the Bhagavad Gita is a jewel. Its importance depends on what we are looking for. Since the purpose of this book is to give a basic understanding of the Bhagavad Gita, thirty-two slokas are taken from various chapters of Bhagavad Gita which can build a basic understanding of its message. These slokas can be memorised as they can help us to redefine our attitude, approach, and vision.

(I) Building the Character: These slokas speak about good and bad characters and their effect on the progress of the individual.

(1) Abhayam Sattva-Sansuddhi Gnāna-Yoga-Vyavasthitih

Dānaṁ damaścha yajñaśhcha svādhyāya stapa arjavam (XVI:1)

(2) Ahimsā satyam akrodhastyāgah santirapaisunam

Dayā bhūteshvaloluptvam mārdavam hrīrachāpalam (XVI.2)

(3) Tejah kṣhamā dhṛitih saucha madroho nātimānitā

Bhavanti sampadam daivīm abhijātasya bhārata (XVI.3)

Fearlessness, purity of heart, steadfastness in acquiring knowledge, the attitude of sharing and giving, control of senses, worshipping the almighty (Yagya), reading scripture being upright (XVI.1)

Being non-violent, being truthful, relinquishing anger, never defaming others, being compassionate towards all beings, not being possessive and greedy, being gentle and not having a fickle mind (XVI.2)

Being energetic, the attitude of bearing and forgiving, not crossing the dharmic limits, being pure, absence of false pride are Divine qualities (XVI.3).

(4) Dambho darpo abhimānascha krodhah pārushyam eva cha

Ajñānam chābhijātasya pārtha sampadam āsurīm (XVI:4)

Ostentation, arrogance, self-deceiving nature, anger, being harsh towards others and ignorance are the qualities of people having demonic qualities (XVI.4).

(5) Daivī sampad vimokṣhāya nibandhāyāsurī matā

Mā suchah sampadam daivīmabhijāto si pāṇḍava (XVI.5)

The Divine qualities promote the progress of the individual whereas the demonic qualities retard the progress. Those who afford to read these stanzas need not have any doubt on 'which category they belong to , the Divine or demonic? They undoubtedly belong to Divine category (XVI.5).

(II). Significance of Sense Control: Following Slokas brings out the significance of self-control.

(6) Trividham narakasyedam dvāram nāśanam ātmanah

Kāmah krodhastathā lobhaha tasmād etat trayam tyajet (XVI:21)

There are three gates to hell and self-ruining. They are Lust, Anger and Greediness. These three need to be relinquished.

(7) Yadā sanharate chāyam kūrmongāni īva sarvasah

Indriyānīnidriyārthebhya stasya pragnā pratistita (XVI:58)

The way a tortoise withdraws its limbs into its shell when it senses the intrusion of the enemy into its habitat, in a similar way one must practice withdrawing senses from distracting forces. This will ensure calmness, and peace of mind. It prepares the mind to ponder over noble things.

(III). Having Patience to Bear Failures and Successes:

(8) Mātrā-sparsāstu kaunteya sītosna -sukha-dukha-dāh

Agamāpāyinonityā stan stitikshasva bhārata (II:14)

Happiness and sorrows come and go in a cyclically like the way summer follows winter and in turn winter follows summer. Have the patience to bear with these cyclic guests. Do not let yourself down during failures. Success will follow if you pursue further based on the lessons you have learnt. Never let the joy of success derail your course. Be alert and keep moving with patience and perseverance.

(IV). Austerities of Speech, Austerity for Heart, and Austerity of Action: How to Practice Tapasya (austerity) with the tools of body and mind are given below

(9) Anudvega-karam vākyam satyam priya-hitam cha yat

Svādhyāyābhyasanam chaiva vāngmayam tapa uchyate (XVII:15)

Speech which does not cause distress to others, which is not only true but also beneficial, which is spoken after thorough study & practice is the austerity of speech. Never misuse the speech to harm or defame others.

(10) Manah-prasādah saumyatvam maunam ātma-vinigrahaha

    Bhāva-sansuddhir ity etat tapo mānasam uchyate (XVII:16)

Practising serenity of heart, being gentle and kind towards all, being silent towards unnecessary things, self -control and refining, strengthening the will -power with pure thoughts is the austerity of heart.

(11) Karmany-evādhikāraste mā phaleshu kadāchana

    Mā karma-phala-hetur bhūr mā te sango stvakarmani (II:45)

You have the right to act, but you don't have the right to the fruits of action. Never identify yourself with the results of action. Never discard action and never cultivate inaction.

(12) Yogasthah kuru karmāni sangam tyaktvā dhanañjaya

    Siddhy-asiddhyoh samo bhūtvā samatvam yoga uchyate (II:48)

Be alert and focused while doing work. Do not let your previous likes and dislikes disturb your focus. Cultivate the attitude of treating both success and failures with the same calmness. This is the ultimate Austerity.

(V) When the Task Ahead is Tough: Never loss your courage. Never withdraw your effort. Believe that you are destined to overpower it.

(13) Klaibyam mā sma gamah pārtha naitat tvayyupapadyate

    Kshudram hridaya-daurbalyam tyaktvottishtha parantapa (II:3)

Never step down from any task out of cowardliness. It does not suit a person like you who is known as a vanquisher. Most heinous among all qualities is having a lack of confidence in yourself. Leave all doubts and apprehensions behind and stand up to face the task.

(VI) For the Soldiers on the Battlefield: Battle is the last resort to uphold order. It comes after all attempts for peace fail. War should be waged to protect humanity from demonic forces.

(14) Hato vā prāpyasi swargam jitvā vā bhokshyase mahīm

   Tasmād uttistha kaunteya yuddhāya krita-nischayaha (II:37)

Stand up firmly to uphold Dharma (duty) by waging war. If you are victorious, you can enjoy the glory of victory. If you die in the war, you will find a place in a heavenly abode.

(15) Swa-dharmam api chāvekshya na vikampitu marhasi

   Dharmyāddhi yuddhā chhreyonyat kshatriyasya na vidyate (II:31)

(16) Yadrichhayā chopapannam swarga-dvāram apāvritam

   Sukhinah kshatriyāh pārtha labhante yuddham īdrisam (II:32)

Never vacillate to execute the defined duty. If your duty calls for waging a war, nothing else suits you other than war (II:31). Lucky are those who get the opportunity to lay their life for Dharma (for a righteous cause). Having washed off all their Karmic dues with the gains made by the noble task that they are involved in where they are ready to sacrifice themselves (surrendered egoistic and selfish causes before a noble cause), these warriors find a place in heaven.

For them, the doors of heaven are wide open (II:32). If you withdraw from the war, you will not only get a bad reputation but also sin (II:33)

(VII) Jeevatma, Prakriti and Paramatma:

(17) Indriyāni parānyāhur indriyebhyah param manah

Manasas tu parā buddhir yo buddheh paratas tu sah (III:42)

Sensory organs are superior in the body, they are supervised by the mind which is superior to the senses. The mind controls the gross and visible. Mind is subordinate to matter-less entities present in the body. They are the feelings & qualities of the individual. Thus, they are superior to the mind. In turn, they are controlled by a further subtle and superior entity called Buddhi (intellect). In turn, intellect is subordinate to Jeevatma (soul) which triggers the feeling of 'I'.

(18) Sarīram yad avāpnoti yatcchāpuyutkrāmatīsavarah

Grihītvaitāni sanyāti vāyur gandhān ivasayāt (XV:8)

Jeevatma doesn't die at the time of death. It carries the aggregate of the qualities that it has experienced while present in the body. As the air carries fragrance from place to place, so does the Jeevatma moves into a new body along with the qualities associated with it from the past life.

(19) Prakritim puruṣham chaiva viddhy anādī ubhāv api

Vikārāns cha gunānsh chaiva viddhi prakritisambhavān (XIII:20)

Jeevatma, Prakriti (Mother Nature) are beginningless. Three primitive qualities or energies namely Satvik, Rajasik, Tamasik, and the avenues for the action are provided by Prakriti.

(20) Anāditvān nirgunatvāt paramātma ayam avyayah

Sarīra-sthopi kaunteya na karoti na lipyate (XIII:31)

(21) Uttamah puruṣhastvanyah paramātmeti udāhritah

Yo loka-trayam āvisya bibharti avyaya īsvaraha (XV:17)

There is a superior entity to Jeevatma present in the body. He is Paramatma. He is not touched by the qualities of the Prakriti. He is above the qualities of Prakriti. He neither acts nor is affected by the results of his acts. He overlooks the activities of Jeevatma (XIII:31).

The higher soul (super soul) that is different from Jeevatma (soul) is called Paramatma. He is pervading all three worlds and sustaining them (XV:17).

Thus, Paramatma is present everywhere both inside our body and outside of the body. We are all immersed in him. There is nothing beyond or nothing subtler than Paramatma. Everything is in him, and he is in everything. The goal of Jeevatma is to reach the abode of Paramatma and behold his vastness and subtleness. Till that state is attained Jeevatma cannot come out of the cycle of birth and death. Seekers follow various paths to attain such a state of liberation.

(VIII). How to Reach the Abode of Paramatma

(22) Dhyānenātmani pasyanti kechid ātmānamātmanā

Anye sānkhyena yogena karma-yogena chāpare (XIII:25)

Any Satvik (nonviolent, pure, compassionate) method can be adopted to reach the abode of the Almighty. Some follow the meditative contemplation to behold the almighty, others through invoking Divinity in the body, mind and soul, some others behold the Almighty through discretionary wisdom on what is temporary and what is permanent through the practice of Sankhya yoga, certain other people practice Karma yoga by offering all their acts at the feet of Almighty. All these methods will lead to the same destination.

(23) Yo yo yām yām tanum bhaktaḥ sraddhayārchitum ichchhati

Tasya tasyāchalām śraddhām tām eva vidadhāmyaham (VII:21)

Whichever form the devotee worships, the Almighty blesses the devotee in that form and strengthens his faith in that form.

(24) Sarva-bhūtastha mātmānam sarva-bhūtāni chātmani

Ikṣhate yoga-yuktātmā sarvatra sama-darsanah (VI:29)

A realised soul starts to see the same Almighty present in all beings and one present in him as the same. He understands and visualises the same Paramatma present in him as being manifested in different forms spread across himself and all other living beings at large.

(IX) We are not Puppets in the Hands of Destiny. Every Individual is his Own Friend or Enemy: Almighty never interferes in our day-to-day life unless sought. Full liberty is given to the individual to choose his own course and bear the fruits of it. The concept of luck or bad luck does not exist in reality. Everything we experience is the result of our own actions and qualities that we nurtured. We are not puppets in the hands of destiny. We are triggering the Law of Karma with our own actions and will.

(25) Uddhared ātmanātmānam nātmānam avasādayet

Atmaiva hyātmano bandhur ātmaiva ripur ātmanah (VI:5)

You must reform and raise on your own. You should not degrade yourself. You are your enemy, or you can be your friend. It is your call how you will use the senses, mind and intellect given to you by Prakriti.

(26) Na kartṛitvaṁ na karmāṇi lokasya sṛijati prabhuh

Na karma-phala-samyogam svabhāvas tu pravartate (V:14)

Almighty neither owns your actions nor triggers you to select any particular nature of actions. He neither delivers on results of actions. People choose their actions on their own based on the qualities that they carry.

(X) Ignorance is not an Excuse: It is essential to dwell deep into the given task and build the required understanding of the task. It is also essential to develop an understanding of the purpose of life and it is essential to set goals for life. We may have to pay a heavy price for ignorance, and callousness towards these tasks.

(27) Ajñasch Asraddadhānas cha sansayātmā vinaśyati

Nāyam lokosti na paro na sukham sansayātmanah (IV:40)

Those who do not develop the knowledge required for the occasion, those who are not sincere in their approach, and those who are fickle-minded will encounter heavy losses. They fail miserably in the physical and spiritual world.

(XI) Surrender at the Feet of Almighty: Almighty can cleanse all our previous Karmic bonds and Sins. He will do it when sought. Till then, he will not interfere as he has given all tools to individuals to reform and raise on their own. Every individual must struggle on his own with the Law of Karma and should overcome bondage to it. However, if any individual seeks the assistance of the Almighty, he will take up the responsibility to elevate us.

(28) Api chet su-durāchāro bhajate mām ananya-bhāk

Sādhur eva sa mantavyah samyag vyavasito hi sah (IX:30)

Even the most dreaded sinner can elevate to a level of sacred and learned monk if he repents for his past sins and resolves firmly to seek the company of Paramatma.

(29) Kṣhipram bhavati dharmātmā sasvach-chhāntim nigachchhati

Kaunteya pratijānīhi na me bhaktah pranasyati (IX:31)

Those who seek my blessings will be transformed into righteous people in an accelerated manner. They will be blessed with lasting peace. Declare *it confidently and loudly to all that, 'those who seek refuge in me will never perish'.*

One must understand that to get cleansed of all past sins, the primary condition is to surrender 'ego'. Once the ego vanishes, past actions cannot find avenues to exist.

(30) Sarva-dharmān parityajya mām ekam saaranam vraja

Aham tvām sarva-pāpebhyo mokṣhayiṣhāmi mā suchah (XVIII:66)

Do not fear, leave all methods of philosophical contemplations, and seek refuge in me. I will wash off all your past sins and liberate you from the cycle of birth and death.

(31) Anan'yāścintayantō māṁ yē janāh paryupāsatē l

Tēsām nityābhiyuktānām yōgakṣēmam vahāmyaham (Gita IX:22)

I take responsibility for the well-being of my devotes who worship me with single-minded devotion. I shower my uninterrupted blessings on them.

(XII) Even a Pinch of Dharma can Save: Many schools of Philosophies were discussed so far. All these schools strive to liberate the individual from ignorance and resultant frustrations Though these schools differ in their understanding of Jeevatma, Prakriti and Paramatma, they all recommend self-reformation to behold the Paramatma present within us and around us. Even a small (Svalpamapi) effort in the direction recommended by any of these philosophical schools can save from perils.

(32) Nehābhikrama-nāśosti pratyavāyo na vidyate

Svalpamapyasya dharmasya trāyate mahato bhayāt (II:40)

The path of Dharma (righteousness) will never result in loss nor give adverse effects. There is no alternative way as well. Even a small effort in the direction recommended by Dharma can save us from great perils

Sanskrit English Word Index

- Adholoka: World of darkness and grief

- Anavopaya: One of the three techniques for focusing the mind in Kashmiri Saivitic yoga

- Anumana: Drawing indirect conclusion.

- Ardhapatti: Knowledge arrived through presumption.

- Atma: Self/Soul/Consciousness independent of body (Jeevatma is also used as equivalent

- Bahu Purusha: Multiple Atmans with independent conscious ness

- Buddhi: Intellect

- Chitta: Mind

- Dahara: The space within the body, Universal cosmic space within the body

- Darshana: Philosophical perception

- Deeksha: Initiation into a religious practice

- Desa: Place

- Dharma: Righteousness, Philosophical opinion

- Gnana/Jnana: Knowledge

- Gunas: Qualities/ Subtle energies of Prakriti

- Guru: Master, Spiritual mentor

- Hatha Yoga: A branch of yoga which focuses to strengthen

body through breathing and postures.

- Jeevatma: Individual Soul

- Karma: Action, Work

- Kauravas: Descendants of King Kuru,

- Klesa: Obstacles, Painful events

- Kutastha: Seating place of supreme consciousness in the body

- Linga: Symbol Indicating Something (An iconic representation of Lord Siva)

- Loka: World

- Mahakala: Lord Siva, one who counts good and bad deeds controls the life span.

- Mahakali: Goddess Parvati, one who annihilates demons.

- Maheswara: The ultimate Divine power (Souls of Souls)

- Manah: Mind

- Mantra: Celestial combination of sounds for chanting, which can help to swim across ignorance, which can invoke Divine consciousness

- Manusha Loka: World where humans are living.

- Maya: Illusion

- Paramatma: Seed soul of all souls, Ultimate Soul

- Peetham/Peetha: Place of Stay of Guru of a sect

- Prajapati: Primordial form of Paramatma, one who made Gods and Creation

- Prakriti: Primordial matter filling the visible and invisible world, Mother Goddess who creates avenues for the evolution of Jeevatma.

- Pralaya: End of Creation.

- Pramana: Correct Knowledge acceptable to all

- Purushottama: Super soul/Paramatma

- Rajasik/Rajo: Second among the three basic qualities, it refers to the drive to act, fierce, restlessness, and strong bonding.

- Rudraksha: Dried seed of Elaeocarpus Ganitrus tree

- Sahasrara: A thousand-petalled subtle energy centre of the body

- Sakti: Goddess of Energy/ Parvati

- Saktopaya: One of the three techniques for focusing the mind in Kashmiri Saivitic yoga.

- Sambhavopaya: One of the three techniques for focusing mind in Kashmiri Saivitic yoga.

- Satva: First one among the three basic qualities, it refers to honesty, purity, truth, compassion, Knowledge and bliss

- Shat: Six

- Sloka: A couplet of Sanskrit verse

- Sutras: Collection of Aphorisms

- Svabhava: Nature

- Tamasa/Tamasik: Third on among the three basic qualities, it refers to Laziness, ignorance, fickle mind, foolishness, dis-honesty, and demonic.

- Tapa: Heat of Austerity
- Yajna/Yagna: A Vedic ritual to invoke Divinity.
- Yama: First step in the eight-fold path of Yoga. It involves purifying body
- Yoga: Technique to calm the agitations of the mind and to focus on the present

Motivation For Writing the Book

As a child, I used to wake up every day listening to Vedic hymns being recited devotionally by my father and the prayer bells rung by my mother. My father who is in his eighties now has been reciting Vedic hymns daily for hours since the times I could recollect. I have never seen him skip the recitation even when he is highly occupied. He got such a staunch devotion not only from the ancestral practices of the family but also from the devotional fervor he imbibed from the holy city of Varanasi where he lived at a young age. He got the opportunity to attend the Vedic schools at Varanasi in the 1950s though for a short duration.

The bold decision taken by my grandfather Sri Ramaiah Ayyavaru who sold all his property and moved from Pamidimukkla (which is a small village in the Krishna district of Andhra Pradesh) to Varanasi always baffles me. The driving force to take such a bold decision to leave his Kith and Kin and move to Varanasi is the desire to live on the banks of the river Ganges, the abode of Goddess Annapurna and Lord Viswanadha. My grandfather also aspired to leave his body in the holy city of Varanasi. Whenever I think over this, I become clueless about what made my grandfather, for that matter, what made lakhs of such seekers risk their life, livelihood, and the future of their families to visit and stay at Varanasi. There was neither the hope of employment nor someone welcoming them with a garland. Yet, over the generations, lakhs of people aspired to reach Varanasi leaving everything behind. They have utmost faith in the Almighty that, he will take care of everything. It is the quest for the eternal truth that propelled generations of seekers towards the holy city of Varanasi. The ghats of the Ganges, the temples of the holy city and the physical presence of Lord Siva and Goddess Annapurneswari in this city attracted those who aspired to know the purpose of life and the delusion of death. My grandfather was one among such innumerable seekers who visited and stayed in this holy city. Such seekers made the holy thoughts flow across India.

In the present social system, the pace of life is getting accelerated. On one hand, children are overloaded with studies and on the other hand, they are also getting distracted due to electronic gadgets. I used to question myself when present-day children enter into the prime time of their life when they encounter challenges of their life, can they show the grit to overcome the challenges? Can they follow the path of Dharma unconditionally at every instance of their life? Will they fight the challenges with the arrows taken from the Dharmic Quiver?

What needs to be done to ensure this? Will they show the same determination to explore the depths of Indian Philosophy that our forefathers have shown? What needs to be done to ensure this?

The property that parents are accumulating may assure assets for children, and the insurances parents take may become handy to children in the hour of crisis, but are the parents insuring anything for the mental and psychological stamina of children ?, When the children grow up, when the challenges are up against them, will they be in a position to subdue the challenges using the time tested treasures of our Philosophy?

Or will they try to reinvent the wheel from their experimentation of trial and error? Answers to most of these questions are ambiguous.

In this background, I thought that there should be a guidebook for everyone to quickly grasp the wisdom of seers. The proposed guidebook should be easy to comprehend. It should carry the essence of Indian Philosophy. It should contain the details on the visible multiplicity of Indian Philosophy, and the freedom provided to choose the path of our choice. It should contain the authentic teachings. Present book is an effort to bring out the essence of my understanding of Indian Philosophical thought that I grasped from my parents and sacred books especially Bhagavad Gita and Patanjali Yoga Sutras.

It is highly recommended for children and elders to memorize the thirty-two slokas presented in the last chapter of this book. These slokas contain the message of the Almighty in his own words. They have the power to transform and benefit everyone who clings to them.

Acknowledgements

This edition is dedicated to my parents Sri Subrahmanya Vara Prasad & Smt Sri Lakshmi. I am their student at school as well as at home. They taught me not only science but also philosophy. My interest in philosophy is due to my Parents. Both motivated me to write this book which is a comprehensive summary of what I learnt from them. For me, they are Like walking Parvati Parameswara (Lord Siva and Goddess Annapurneswari). Their severe austerities and strong devotion towards Lord Siva are an inspiration for me.

I thank my wife Padmavathi whose encouragement and continuous support over the years enabled me to spend more time in my professional and spiritual life. Without her support, my plan to bring out this book would not have culminated into a reality. Special thanks to my daughters Aparna and Vagdevi. They learnt how not to disturb me when I am dwelling deep into philosophical writings.

I express my sincere thanks to my brothers Sri I B Phani Ram and Sri Umakanth who are my spiritual companions. Their encouragement and blessings are present subtly in this book.

I convey my special thanks to my maternal uncle late Sri Yaddanapudi Venkateswara Rao for his encouragement to bring out a book with my thoughts on Bhagavad Gita.

Special thanks to my friends D Kondaiah, and Eswar Raju who encouraged me during the writing of this book.

Thanks to M/s Deep Dark Creations for the artwork and illustrations. Special thanks to Ms Rashmi K from freelancer.com for the cover page design. I express my thanks to Ms Mannu Sharma for making some of the illustrations in this book.

I acknowledge Almighty for blessing me to incline towards philosophical explorations and triggering my thoughts to take up this task. I humbly offer the outcome of this effort at his feet.

Made in the USA
Monee, IL
26 June 2023

37603290R00125